Deploying OpenStack

Deploying OpenStack

Ken Pepple

Beijing · Cambridge · Farnham · Köln · Sebastopol · Tokyo

Deploying OpenStack

by Ken Pepple

Published by O'Reilly Media, Inc., 1005 Gravenstein Highway North, Sebastopol, CA 95472.

O'Reilly books may be purchased for educational, business, or sales promotional use. Online editions are also available for most titles (*http://my.safaribooksonline.com*). For more information, contact our corporate/institutional sales department: (800) 998-9938 or *corporate@oreilly.com*.

Editors: Mike Loukides and Meghan Blanchette
Production Editor: O'Reilly Publishing Services

Cover Designer: Karen Montgomery
Interior Designer: David Futato
Illustrator: O'Reilly Publishing Services

Printing History:

July 2011:   First Edition.

ISBN: 978-1-449-31105-6

[LSI]

1311280420

Table of Contents

Preface

This book is aimed at developers, technologists, and system administrators eager to understand and deploy cloud computing infrastructure projects based upon OpenStack software. It is intended to provide the reader with a solid understanding of the Open-Stack project goals, details of specific OpenStack software components, general design decisions, and detailed steps to deploy OpenStack in a few controlled scenarios. Along the way, readers would also learn common pitfalls in architecting, deploying, and implementing their cloud.

Intended Audience

This book assumes that the reader is familiar with public Infrastructure as a Service (IaaS) cloud offerings such as Rackspace Cloud or Amazon Web Services. In addition, it demands an understanding of Linux systems administration, such as installing servers, networking with iptables, and basic virtualization technologies.

Conventions Used in This Book

The following typographical conventions are used in this book:

Italic
> Indicates new terms, URLs, email addresses, filenames, and file extensions.

`Constant width`
> Used for program listings, as well as within paragraphs to refer to program elements such as variable or function names, databases, data types, environment variables, statements, and keywords.

`Constant width bold`
> Shows commands or other text that should be typed literally by the user.

`Constant width italic`
> Shows text that should be replaced with user-supplied values or by values determined by context.

This icon signifies a tip, suggestion, or general note.

 This icon indicates a warning or caution.

Using Code Examples

This book is here to help you get your job done. In general, you may use the code in this book in your programs and documentation. You do not need to contact us for permission unless you're reproducing a significant portion of the code. For example, writing a program that uses several chunks of code from this book does not require permission. Selling or distributing a CD-ROM of examples from O'Reilly books does require permission. Answering a question by citing this book and quoting example code does not require permission. Incorporating a significant amount of example code from this book into your product's documentation does require permission.

We appreciate, but do not require, attribution. An attribution usually includes the title, author, publisher, and ISBN. For example: "*Deploying OpenStack* by Ken Pepple (O'Reilly). Copyright 2011 Ken Pepple, 978-1-449-31105-6."

If you feel your use of code examples falls outside fair use or the permission given above, feel free to contact us at *permissions@oreilly.com*.

Safari® Books Online

 Safari Books Online is an on-demand digital library that lets you easily search over 7,500 technology and creative reference books and videos to find the answers you need quickly.

With a subscription, you can read any page and watch any video from our library online. Read books on your cell phone and mobile devices. Access new titles before they are available for print, and get exclusive access to manuscripts in development and post feedback for the authors. Copy and paste code samples, organize your favorites, download chapters, bookmark key sections, create notes, print out pages, and benefit from tons of other time-saving features.

O'Reilly Media has uploaded this book to the Safari Books Online service. To have full digital access to this book and others on similar topics from O'Reilly and other publishers, sign up for free at *http://my.safaribooksonline.com*.

How to Contact Us

Please address comments and questions concerning this book to the publisher:

O'Reilly Media, Inc.
1005 Gravenstein Highway North
Sebastopol, CA 95472
800-998-9938 (in the United States or Canada)
707-829-0515 (international or local)
707-829-0104 (fax)

We have a web page for this book, where we list errata, examples, and any additional information. You can access this page at:

http://www.oreilly.com/catalog/9781449311056

To comment or ask technical questions about this book, send email to:

bookquestions@oreilly.com

For more information about our books, courses, conferences, and news, see our website at *http://www.oreilly.com*.

Find us on Facebook: *http://facebook.com/oreilly*

Follow us on Twitter: *http://twitter.com/oreillymedia*

Watch us on YouTube: *http://www.youtube.com/oreillymedia*

Acknowledgments

In general, I would like to thank the entire OpenStack community that gathers on the #openstack IRC channel, mail aliases, and forums. The help and encouragement from hoards of people I might never meet face-to-face has been of immeasurable value. Thank you.

More specifically, I would like to thank many people for their help both in the past and the present that led me to this place:

- A special thanks to Josh Kearney for collaborating with me on my first Nova blueprint, as well as technically reviewing this book.
- Jay Pipes, for walking me through my first halting few commits and his leadership of Glance.
- Vishvananda Ishaya, for generally being a fountain of cloud knowledge and for his technical leadership of the Nova project.
- Anne Gentle, for spearheading the awesome OpenStack wiki and documentation.

- The people at Cloudscaling, who have been helping customers around the world deploy OpenStack clouds. A special thanks to Francesco Paolo and Andrew Shafer for their support.
- Brian Pepple, for his technical review of the book, as well as his introduction to open source development.
- Diego Parrilla and the team at StackOps, for access to their distribution and for their technical review of the book.
- The fine people at Spark and Associates, especially Joon Lee, Nick Lee, and Sung Park.
- Shlomo Swidler, for insights into cloud infrastructures at levels above where I usually contemplate.
- Dan Sanderson, who unlocked the riddle of using Scrivener, DocBook, Python, and subversion in harmony for me.
- All the great people that I worked with at Sun Microsystems over the years, especially Dr. James Baty, Jason Carolan, John Stanford, SeChang Oh, Bonghwan Kim, Richard Qualls, Scott Radeztsky, Brad Vaughan, Ken Buchanan, Jeff McIver, Edward Wustenhoff, Neeladri Bose, Bill Walker, and Gary Kelly. Many of them were pioneering dynamic infrastructures long ago and profoundly influenced my thinking along the way.

Finally, but certainly not least, thanks to my amazing partner, Shelley, for her love and support.

## CHAPTER 1

The OpenStack Project

The OpenStack project has been created with the audacious goal of being the ubiquitous software choice for building cloud infrastructures. In just over one year, it has gone from an idea to start collaborating to being the most talked-about project in open source. In this chapter, we will examine the project's goals, history, and how you can participate in its future.

What Is the OpenStack Project ?

The OpenStack Project aims to create an open source cloud computing platform for public and private clouds aimed at scalability without complexity. Initially focusing on Infrastructure as a Service (IaaS) offerings, the project currently encompasses three components:

- OpenStack Compute: Software to orchestrate, manage, and offer virtual machines. The software for this is called "Nova."
- OpenStack Object Store: Software for the redundant storage of static objects. The software for this is called "Swift."
- OpenStack Image Service: Provides query and storage services for virtual disk images. The software for this is called "Glance."

One of the defining core values behind the project is its embrace of openness with both open standards and open source code. OpenStack has been released under the Apache 2.0 license. If you are unfamiliar with the license, you should review the full license (*http://www.apache.org/licenses/LICENSE-2.0.html*) or skip to the layman's terms (*http://www.apache.org/foundation/licence-FAQ.html#WhatDoesItMEAN*). In addition, OpenStack promotes open standards through the OpenStack API.

The OpenStack project began through the work of two organizations: Rackspace Hosting (a large US hosting firm) and NASA (the US Space agency) decided to join forces and release their internal cloud object storage and cloud compute code bases (respectively) as a common open source project.

These releases were the basis for OpenStack Object Storage ("Swift") and OpenStack Compute ("Nova") projects. After the first release, another project (named "Glance") was added to handle image storage. Currently, these are the only official components of the OpenStack project.

Releases

The code was first posted in July of 2010, and the first release (nicknamed "Austin") was released to the public in November 2010. Following a short three-month development cycle, the second release (codenamed "Bexar" but pronounced "Bear") debuted in February 2011, followed by "Cactus" in April, 2011.

 Release names are decided by popular vote by the community of developers from a pool of city names near the site of the next OpenStack Developers Summit. For example, The Diablo release was named after Diablo, California, which is (somewhat) near Santa Clara, California, the site of the 2011 Spring OpenStack Developer Summit. In late June 2011, the developers choose the name "Essex" for the fifth release of OpenStack. Essex, Massachusetts is about 30 miles north of Boston, the announced site for the Fall 2011 OpenStack Developers Summit.

Table 1-1 shows OpenStack releases and the corresponding software versions.

Table 1-1. OpenStack Releases

Release	Date	Versions
Austin	October 21, 2010	OpenStack Nova 2010.1 (*http://launchpad.net/nova/austin/2010.1*)
		OpenStack Swift 1.1.0 (*http://launchpad.net/swift/austin/2010.1*)
Bexar	February 3, 2011	Nova 2011.1 (*https://launchpad.net/nova/bexar/2011.1*)
		Glance 0.1.7 (*https://launchpad.net/glance/bexar/0.1.7*)
		OpenStack Swift 1.2.0 (*https://launchpad.net/swift/1.2/1.2.0*)
Cactus	April 15, 2011	OpenStack Nova 2011.2 (*https://launchpad.net/nova/cactus/2011.2*)
		OpenStack Glance 2011.2 (*https://launchpad.net/glance/cactus/2011.2*)
		OpenStack Swift 1.3.0 (*https://launchpad.net/swift/1.3/1.3.0*)
Diablo	September 22, 2011 (proposed)	To be determined
Essex	To be determined	To be determined

You can always see a list of all (past and future) releases at *http://wiki.openstack.org/Releases*.

Community

Much is made of the large community aspect of OpenStack, and with great reason: the community was created by end users (cloud service providers and large enterprise) with the active participation of large computing vendors and many other open source projects. In less than a year, OpenStack has become arguably the largest open source cloud project.

At the end of June 2010, the OpenStack community boasted 217 registered developers and 80 contributing companies. These 217 registered developers have been very active. In just the month of June 2010, OpenStack Compute (Nova) had 1,382 commits by 65 people, OpenStack Object Storage (Swift) had 101 commits by 12 people, and OpenStack Image Registry (Glance) had 164 commits by 12 people.

The OpenStack community is extremely active and maintains many outlets for information about the project:

- Forums for active discussions on all OpenStack projects are located at *http://forums.openstack.org/*.
- The OpenStack wiki is hosted at *http://wiki.openstack.org/StartingPage* and is updated almost daily with new information.
- The official documentation for each of the OpenStack project releases is available at *http://docs.openstack.org/*.
- Mailing lists for OpenStack are detailed at *http://wiki.openstack.org/MailingLists*. Each of the lists are targeted to different audiences and have different volumes of email.
- Launchpad is the current home for source control and project management and is located at *https://launchpad.net/nova*. In the future, the codebase may be moving to *http://github.com/*.
- Blog posts from OpenStack developers and prominent community members are aggregated at *http://planet.openstack.org/*.
- Active, real-time discussion about OpenStack projects are held on IRC on the #openstack (general OpenStack discussions) and #openstack-dev (developer-oriented OpenStack discussion) on Freenode at *irc://freenode.net/*. As noted in the documentation, "This is usually the best place to ask questions and find your way around. IRC stands for Internet Relay Chat and it is a way to chat online in real time. You can also ask a question and come back to the log files to read the answer later." The logs are available at *http://eavesdrop.openstack.org/irclogs/*.

## CHAPTER 2

Understanding Swift

Swift is the oldest and probably the mature project within OpenStack. It is the underlying technology that powers Rackspace's Cloud Files™ (*http://www.rackspace.com/cloud/cloud_hosting_products/files/*) service. While it only interacts tangentially with Nova (as shown in Chapter 3), it is still important in the overall scheme of understanding OpenStack.

Swift aims to provide a massively scalable and redundant object store conceptually similar to Amazon's S3 service. To provide this scalability and redundancy, it writes multiple copies of each object to multiple storage servers within separate "zones." Zones are a logical grouping of storage servers that have been isolated from each other to guard against failures. The level of isolation is up to the cloud operator; they can be isolated on differing servers (ability to lose individual servers), different racks (ability to lose entire rack), different sections of the data center, or even different data centers. Each choice provides a different level of isolation and cost.

Many beginners assume that Swift will take the place of their file server and that they will be able to easily mount volumes on their desktops to access their files. This is not the case. Swift is an object store, not a file server. While these sound similar, there are important differences. Object stores simply save files in logical groupings (called "containers" in Swift parlance) via a RESTful protocol. They do not provide a true filesystem, nor are they accessible through standard file sharing protocols like NFS (Network File System, the standard for UNIX), CIFS (Common Internet File System, the standard for Windows), or AFS (Appleshare Files System, the standard for Mac OS X). To access your files, you will need to use a the Swift API client. These are described later in this chapter.

Swift is configurable in terms of how many copies (called "replicas") are written, as well as how many zones are configured. Current best practices call for three replicas written across five zones. As the number of replicas is less than or equal to the number of zones, Swift tries to balance the writing of objects to storage servers so that the write and read load is distributed. This is illustrated in Figure 2-1.

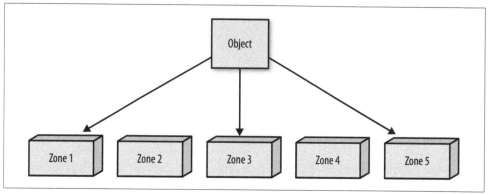

Figure 2-1. Swift Replicas And Zones

Architecture

The logical view of Swift can be divided into two logical parts: presentation and resource. The major components, data stores, and interactions are illustrated in Figure 2-2.

Presentation

Swift accepts end user requests via *swift-proxy* processes. *swift-proxy* accepts incoming end user requests; optionally authorizes and authenticates them; then passes them on to the appropriate object, account, or container processes for completion. It can optionally work with a cache (*memcached**) to reduce authentication, container, and account calls. *swift-proxy* accepts requests via the OpenStack API on port 80. There is also an optional middleware to support the Amazon S3 protocol.

Authentication

Swift handles authentication through a three-step process:

- User authenticates through the authentication system (or middleware within *swift-proxy*) and receives a unique token (which is an operator-customizable string). This step is only required if the user doesn't possess a valid token. Tokens are valid for an operator-configurable time limit (Rackspace Cloud Files™ uses a 24-hour timeout).

---

* Memcached is a free and open-source in-memory key-value store for caching small pieces of data.

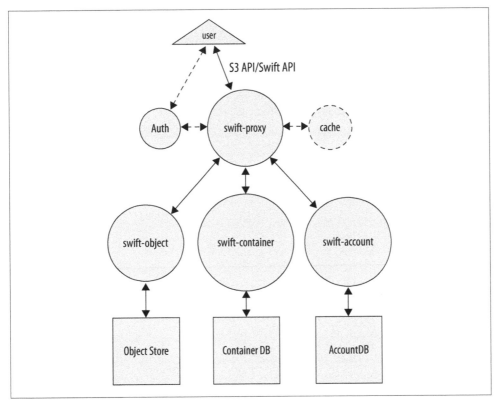

Figure 2-2. Swift Logical Architecture

- User issues a second request to Swift (directly to *swift-proxy*), passing the token along with the request in the HTTP headers.

- *swift-proxy* validates the token and responds to user request with the help of *swift-account*, *swift-container*, and/or *swift-object*.

Swift authentication can be implemented through WSGI middleware or as a separate system. For most installations, the WSGI middleware option will be more straightforward. However, some enterprises might find the separate system approach easier to integrate to their current authentication scheme. Swift ships with sample authentication code called swauth, which stores the authentication database within Swift itself.

Resource

Swift manages a number of information sources through three processes that fulfill requests from *swift-proxy*. These three daemons are:

- *swift-account*, which manages a sqlite3 database of accounts defined with the object storage service.

- *swift-container* manages another sqlite3 database, but contains a mapping of containers (analogous to buckets in Amazon's S3) within the object store service.
- *swift-object*, a mapping of actual objects (i.e., Files) stored on the storage node.

Each of these processes are responsible for fulfilling requests from the proxy node, as well as auditing their own mappings (database consistency) and replicating any inconsistent information to other nodes in the ring.

## CHAPTER 3

Understanding Glance

Glance is the newest OpenStack service. First debuting in the Bexar release, Glance provides a catalog service for storing and querying virtual disk images. Glance has been designed to be a standalone service for those needing to organize large sets of virtual disk images. However, when used along with Nova and Swift, it provides an end-to-end solution for cloud disk image management.

Architecture

There are three pieces to Glance architecture: *glance-api*, *glance-registry*, and the image store. As you can probably guess, *glance-api* accepts API calls, much like *nova-api*, and the actual image blobs are placed in the image store. The *glance-registry* stores and retrieves metadata about images. The image store can be a number of different object stores, including Swift. Figure 3-1 illustrates Glance's logical architecture.

glance-api is similar in functionality to *nova-api*, in that it accepts incoming API requests and then communicates with the other components (*glance-registry* and the image store) to facilitate querying, retrieving, uploading, or deleting images. By default, *glance-api* listens on port 9292.

In the Cactus release, Glance lacks authentication and authorization, making it unsuitable for direct end user usage except in tightly controlled environments. The best way to use this is "behind" Nova, where *nova-api* authenticates and authorizes requests for uploading, querying, and using virtual disk images.

The *glance-registry* process stores and retrieves metadata about images. The version that ships with Glance is only considered a reference implementation, as most large installations will want a customized version for their service. The reference version uses sqlite3 to store the metadata and the Glance API for communications. By default, *glance-registry* listens on port 9191.

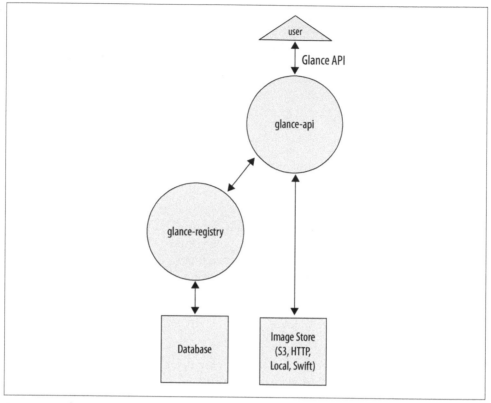

Figure 3-1. Glance Logical Architecture

The Glance database contains only two tables: Image and Image Property. The image table represents the image in the datastore (disk format, container format, size, etc.), while the Image Property table contains custom image metadata. While the image representation and image metadata is stored in the database, the actual images are stored in image stores.

Image stores are the storage places for the virtual disk image and come in a number of different options. The currently supported image stores are shown in Table 3-1.

Table 3-1. Glance Image Store Options

Image Store	Description
Fileystem	Stores, deletes, and gets images from a filesystem directory specified in the configuration file (`filesystem_store_datadir` option). This could be a filesystem on a shared drive (e.g., NFS).
HTTP	Retrieves images from a URL. This is a read-only image store option. Images will need to be saved to the URL via another mechanism.
Swift	Stores, deletes, and gets images from a Swift installation. Requires several configuration options in *glance.conf*.
S3	Deletes or gets images (but not stores) from Amazon's S3 service.

Each of these options have their own strengths and weaknesses. However, most large installations will use Swift, while smaller installations will probably gravitate to the simplicity of the filesystem option with a shared NFS server. The S3 or HTTP image stores are probably only useful for referencing publicly available images.

With this overview of Glance, it should now be clear how Glance provides the "glue" between Swift and Nova. Figure 3-2 shows the interactions between OpenStack projects for virtual disk image storage and retrieval.

Figure 3-2. OpenStack Image Ecosystem

Image Support

Glance supports a wide array of virtual disk and container formats. Virtual disks are analogous to a physical server's boot drives, only condensed into a file. Different virtualization technologies support different disk formats. Glance supports the disk formats shown in Table 3-2.

Table 3-2. Glance Supported Disk Formats

Disk Format	Notes
Raw	Unstructured disk format
VHD	Most common format supported by most OpenStack virtualization technologies except KVM.
VMDK	Format popularized by VMware.
qcow2	QEMU image format, native format for KVM and QEMU. Supports advanced functions.
VDI	Virtual disk image format originated by Oracle VM VirtualBox.
ISO	Archive format for optical disks.
AMI, ARI, AKI	Amazon machine, ramdisk, and kernel images (respectively). See more information at the Amazon EC2 User Guide (*http://docs.amazonwebservices.com/AWSEC2/latest/UserGuide/index.html?ComponentsAMIs.html*).

Glance also supports the concept of container formats, which describes the file format and contains additional metadata. Glance supports two container formats as well as the absence of a container format (bare), as shown in Table 3-3.

Table 3-3. Glance Container Formats

Container Format	Notes
OVF	An open standard for distributing one or more virtual machine images. Read more about this standard at *http://www.dmtf.org/standards/ovf*.

Container Format	Notes
aki, ari, ami	Amazon kernel, ramdisk, or machine image (respectively). Read more about these container formats at Amazon EC2 User Guide (*http://docs.amazonwebservices.com/AWSEC2/latest/UserGuide/index.html?ComponentsAMIs.html*).
Bare	No container for this image.

API Support

The Glance API is a simple REST API for querying image metadata or storing or retrieving actual images. Data is returned as a JSON-encoded (*http://www.json.org/*) mapping (query) or binary (image retrieval). Below is an example of querying Glance using *curl* for details on all images:

```
$ curl http://localhost:9292/images
{"images":
    [{"name": "natty-uec",
       "container_format": "ami",
       "disk_format": "ami",
       "checksum": "b420e097baf54cd32af5970b3f0cb93b",
       "id": 6,
       "size": 1476395008}]
}
```

In this example, Glance shows that there is only one image in the registry.

 The List Images and List Images Detail calls can return huge amounts of data for large image stores, as no record filtering exists in this version of Glance.

The Glance API calls are detailed in Table 3-4.

Table 3-4. Glance API Calls

Action	API Call	Description
Store Image	POST /images	Stores the image and then returns the metadata created about it
Download Image	GET /images/ID	Retrieves image specified by ID
Update Image	PUT /images/ID	Update image metadata or actual data specified by ID
Delete Image	DELETE /images/ID	Delete image specified by ID
List Images	GET /images	Return id, name, disk_format, container_format, checksum, and size of all images
List Images Detail	GET /images/detail	Return list (with all metadata) of all images
Image Details	HEAD /images/ID	Return all metadata for image specified by ID

The full API documentation can be viewed at the online documentation website (*http://docs.openstack.org/cactus/openstack-compute/admin/content/openstack-imaging-service-glance-rest-api.html*).

Installation

If you are on Ubuntu 11.04 or later, Glance can be installed with a simple apt-get:

```
$ sudo apt-get install glance python-glance-doc
```

 Glance requires a large number of dependencies.

Once installed, it needs to be started with the *glance-control* utility.

```
$ sudo glance-control all start
```

Glance is now ready for uploading and querying of virtual disk images. The *glance index* command shows all virtual disk images currently in Glance.

```
$ glance index
No public images found.
```

As you can see from the example above, Glance is currently empty. Let's put a image into it. The *glance-upload* command puts an image record into the *glance-registry* and stores the data file in the image store. It requires a the disk format and container format as a minimum set of arguments. In this example, the virtual disk is formatted as an AMI from the Ubuntu Enterprise Cloud image repository (*http://uec-images.ubuntu.com/releases/natty/release/*).

```
$ glance-upload natty-server-uec-amd64.img natty-uec --disk-format ami \
  --container-format ami
Stored image. Got identifier: {u'checksum': u'b420e097baf54cd32af5970b3f0cb93b',
u'container_format': u'ami',
u'created_at': u'2011-07-06T00:54:23.600181',
u'deleted': False,
u'deleted_at': None,
u'disk_format': u'ami',
u'id': 6,
u'is_public': True,
u'location': u'file:///var/lib/glance/images/6',
u'name': u'natty-uec',
u'properties': {u'type': u'raw'},
u'size': 1476395008,
u'status': u'active',
u'updated_at': u'2011-07-06T00:55:01.901066'}
```

Now that an image has been uploaded, Glance should show it via the *glance index* command.

```
$ glance index
Found 1 public images...
ID   Name        Disk Format  Container Format    Size
--   ----------  ------------ -------------------- --------------
6    natty-uec   ami          ami                 1476395008
```

The *glance show* command is able to show details about the newly uploaded image.

```
$ glance show 6
URI: http://0.0.0.0/images/6
Id: 6
Public: Yes
Name: natty-uec
Size: 1476395008
Location: file:///var/lib/glance/images/6
Disk format: ami
Container format: ami
Property 'type': raw
```

This image is now available for use.

## CHAPTER 4

Understanding Nova

Nova seeks to provide a framework for the large-scale provisioning and management of virtual compute instances. Similar in functionality and scope to Amazon's EC2 service, it allows you to create, manage, and destroy virtual servers based on your own system images through a programmable API.

Nova Architecture

Nova is architected as a distributed application with many components, but the majority of these are custom-written Python daemons of two varieties:

- Web Server Gateway Interface (WSGI)* applications to receive and mediate API calls
- Worker daemons to carry out orchestration tasks

However, there are two essential pieces of the architecture that are neither custom written nor Python-based: the messaging queue and the database. These two components facilitate the asynchronous orchestration of complex tasks through message passing and information sharing. Piecing this all together we get a picture like Figure 4-1.

This complicated diagram can be summed up in three sentences:

- End users who want to use Nova to create compute instances call *nova-api* with OpenStack API or EC2 API requests.
- Nova daemons exchange information through the queue (actions) and database (information) to carry out these API requests.
- Glance is a completely separate service that Nova interfaces through the Glance API to provide virtual disk imaging services.

---

* WSGI is a Python standard specification that defines the communications between web and application servers.

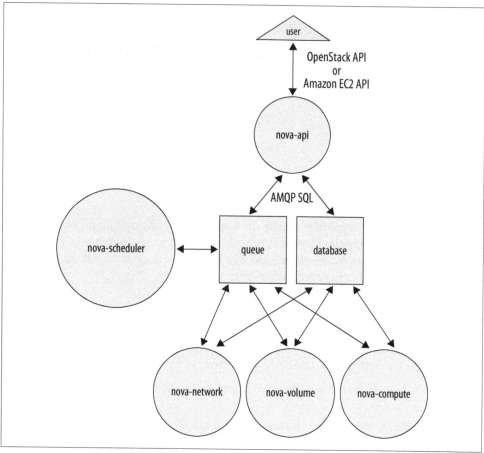

Figure 4-1. Nova Logical Architecture

Now that we've seen the overview of the processes and their interactions, let's take a closer look at each component.

API

The *nova-api* daemon is the heart of Nova. You may see it illustrated on many pictures of Nova as API and "Cloud Controller." While this is partly true, cloud controller is really just a class (specifically the CloudController in *nova/api/ec2/cloud.py*) within the *nova-api* daemon. Its primary purpose is to accept and fulfill incoming API requests.

To accept and fulfill API requests, *nova-api* provides an endpoint for all API queries (accepting requests using either the OpenStack API or the Amazon EC2 API), initiates most of the orchestration activities (such as running an instance), and also enforces some policy (mostly quota checks). For some requests, it will fulfill the entire request itself by querying the database and then returning the answer. For more complicated requests, it will pass messages to other daemons through a combination of writing information to the database and adding messages to the queue.

By default, *nova-api* listens on port 8773 for the EC2 API and 8774 for the OpenStack API.

Scheduler

The *nova-scheduler* process is conceptually the simplest piece of code in Nova: it takes a virtual machine instance request from the queue and determines where it should run (specifically, which compute server host it should run on). In practice, however, this will grow to be the most complex piece, as it needs to factor in the current state of the entire cloud infrastructure and apply complicated algorithms to ensure efficient usage. To that end, *nova-scheduler* implements a pluggable architecture that lets you choose (or write) your own algorithm for scheduling. Table 4-1 details the current scheduler choices.

Table 4-1. Nova Schedulers

Scheduler	Notes
Simple	Attempts to find least loaded host.
Chance	Chooses random available host from service table. This is the default scheduler.
Zone	Picks random host from within an availability zone.

To illustrate how simple *nova-scheduler* can be, here is the relevant code from the chance scheduler class in *nova/schedule/chance.py*:

```
class ChanceScheduler(driver.Scheduler):
    """Implements Scheduler as a random node selector."""

    def schedule(self, context, topic, *_args, **_kwargs):
        """Picks a host that is up at random."""

        hosts = self.hosts_up(context, topic)
        if not hosts:
            raise driver.NoValidHost(_("Scheduler was unable to locate a host"
                                       " for this request. Is the appropriate"
                                       " service running?"))
        return hosts[int(random.random() * len(hosts))]
```

As you can see from above code sample, the schedule method simply chooses a random host from the array of hosts that are currently known to be "up."

Compute Worker

The *nova-compute* process is primarily a worker daemon that creates and terminates virtual machine instances. The process by which it does so is fairly complex, but the basics are simple: accept actions from the queue and then perform one or a series of virtual machine API calls to carry them out while updating state in the database. An example of this would be *nova-compute* accepting a message from the queue to create a new instance and then using the `libvirt` library to start a new KVM instance.

There are a variety of ways that *nova-compute* manages virtual machines. The most common is through a software package called `libvirt`. This is a toolkit (API, daemon, and utilities) created by Red Hat to interact with the capabilities of a wide range of Linux virtualization technologies. While `libvirt` may be the most common, *nova-compute* also uses the Xen API, vSphere API, Windows Management Interface, and others to support other virtualization technologies.

One of strengths of Nova is its wide support for virtualization technologies. The virtualization technologies supported in the current release version of Nova are detailed in Table 4-2.

Table 4-2. Virtualization Support in Nova

Virtuali-zation Product	Sup-ported	Interface	Support Notes
Kernel Virtual Machine (KVM)	Yes	libvirt	Most popular technology for small scale deployments. Arguably the easiest to deploy and configure. Supports advanced operations such as live migration and resize.
Xen	Yes	libvirt	Most popular (along with XCP/XenServer) technology for larger scale and production deployments.
Citrix XenServer	Yes	XenAPI	Citrix's commercial version of Xen-based virtualization product. Supports advanced features.
Xen Cloud Platform (XCP)	Yes	XenAPI	The open source version of Citrix XenServer available under the LGPL, GPL, Q Public License v1. Supports subset of XenServer features.
VMware ESX / ESXi / vSphere	Yes	vSphere API	Most popular enterprise virtualization platform. See the OpenStack VMware documentation (*http://nova.openstack.org/vmwareapi_readme.html*) for full information and restrictions when using this option.
VMware vSphere	No		
User Mode Linux	Yes	libvirt	Generally considered a lower performance virtualization option, UML runs each guest as a regular process in user space.
Microsoft Hyper-V	Yes	Windows Management Instrumentation (WMI)	Hyper-V is Microsoft's hypervisor-based virtualization technology.
QEMU	Yes	libvirt	Provides the basis for most Linux-based virtualization technologies (such as KVM and Virtualbox).

Virtuali-zation Product	Sup-ported	Interface	Support Notes
Linux Containers (LXC)	Yes	libvirt	LXC is an operating system-level partitioning technology that allows for running multiple isolated servers (containers) in a single kernel. LXC does not actually virtualize the server. Instead, it provides a virtual environment with its own process space. While this doesn't provide the same level of isolation (as every partition shares the common kernel), it may provide some advantages in I/O performance.
Oracle VM VirtualBox	No		

"Virtualization Technology" on page 31 describes some important considerations that should be taken into account when choosing your virtualization technology.

Volume Worker

As you can gather by the name, *nova-volume* manages the creation, attaching, and detaching of persistent volumes to compute instances (similar in functionality to Amazon's Elastic Block Storage (*http://aws.amazon.com/ebs/*)). It can use volumes from a variety of providers such as iSCSI or AoE. Table 4-3 shows the current volume provider options.

Table 4-3. Nova Volume Provider Options

Volume Provider	Notes
AoE	High performance layer 2 Ethernet technology that encapsulates SATA commands in Ethernet frames. Supported on Linux through the AoE Tools package, specifically the vblade program (*http://sourceforge.net/projects/aoe tools/*).
iSCSI	A commonly used IP-based encapsulation of SCSI commands. This is supported by most modern operating systems, but the Nova implementation only currently supports Linux through with this implementation. This driver does support CHAP for authentication.
Solaris iSCSI	Supports Solaris-hosted iSCSI volumes and uses ZFS commands. Solaris server must be prepared by following the instructions in the *nova/volume/san.py* file.
Sheepdog	An open-source, distributed storage system specifically designed for QEMU/KVM installations that is developed by NTT Laboratories. More information is available at *http://www.osrg.net/sheepdog/*.
RBD	RADOS block device (RBD) driver to interact with Ceph, a distributed file system based on a reliable and scalable distributed object store. As stated on *http://ceph.newdream.net/* the wiki, "Ceph is under heavy development, and is not yet suitable for any uses other than benchmarking and review."
LeftHand	A driver for interacting with HP Lefthand SAN solutions (as of now known as "HP P4000 SAN Solutions"). Unlike other providers mentioned above, this provider does not run directly on the SAN hardware. Instead, it accesses it via *SSH* commands.

Network Worker

The *nova-network* worker daemon is very similar to *nova-compute* and *nova-volume*. It accepts networking tasks from the queue and then performs system commands to manipulate the network (such as setting up bridging interfaces or changing *iptables* rules).

Nova defines two different types of IP addresses for an instance: Fixed IPs and Floating IPs. These can be broadly thought of as private IPs (fixed) and public IPs (floating). Fixed IPs are assigned on instance startup and remain the same during their entire lifetimes. Floating IPs are dynamically allocated and associated to a domain to allow outside connectivity.

To support the assignment and connectivity of fixed IPs, Nova supports three networking managers:

- Flat is the most basic network manager. Each new instance is assigned a fixed IP address and attached to a common bridge (which must be created by the administrator). IP configuration information must be "injected" (written into the new instance virtual disk image) to configure the instance.

- FlatDHCP builds upon the Flat manager by providing DHCP services to handle instance addressing and creation of bridges.

- VLAN supports that most features. In this mode, *nova-network* creates a VLAN, a subnet, and a separate bridge for each project. Each project also receives a range of IP only accessible within the VLAN.

Of these three network managers, VLAN is the most featured, Flat is the most barebones (but flexible), and FlatDHCP strikes a nice balance between the two.

Queue

The queue provides a central hub for passing messages between daemons. This is currently implemented with RabbitMQ (*http://www.rabbitmq.com/*) today, but theoretically could be any AMPQ message queue (*http://www.amqp.org/confluence/display/AMQP/Advanced+Message+Queuing+Protocol*) supported by the Python ampqlib (*http://barryp.org/software/py-amqplib/*) and carrot (*http://ask.github.com/carrot/*) libraries.

Nova creates several types of message queues to facilitate communication between the various daemons. These include: topics queues, fanout queues, and host queues. Topics queues allow messages to be broadcast to the number of particular class of worker daemons. For example, Nova uses these to pass messages to all (or any) of the compute or volume daemons. This allows Nova to use the first available worker to process the message. Host queues allow Nova to send messages to specific services on specific hosts. For example, Nova often needs to send a message to a specific host's compute worker to take action on a particular instance. Fanout queues are only currently used for the advertising of the service capabilities to *nova-scheduler* workers.

Here is an example of the queues created in RabbitMQ for a simple all-in-one node installation:

```
$ sudo rabbitmqctl list_queues
Listing queues ...
scheduler_fanout_15b1731c5ac34aae8970369911f04542  0
volume     0
volume_fanout_e42438faedb84ab8aad8d85e29916424  0
compute_fanout_38a37d3dc7564b66a5a540a1e222b12b  0
compute.cactus  0
volume_fanout_d62eb016a76341f4899c91d5a8fbb0a9  0
volume_fanout_dcaebd5edb3045ff8b86636040d34071  0
volume.cactus  0
network_fanout_64b9cb80b2c34c7a8da983219c787147  0
compute     0
network_fanout_362393151e7c465a8e3ed003ac6dbc1b  0
compute_fanout_74165ee38c9d4c1ea1003ccd88a91c22  0
scheduler     0
network.cactus  0
network     0
scheduler_fanout_9444b4c8d5d6497b9b5e2df4eca33b0d  0
scheduler.cactus  0
```

As you can see from the example, topic, fanout, and host queues have been created for each service (*nova-scheduler*, *nova-compute*, *nova-volume*, *nova-network*).

Database

The database stores most of the configuration and run-time state for a cloud infrastructure. This includes the instance types that are available for use, instances in use, networks available, and projects. Table 4-4 details all the tables in the current Nova database scheme.

Table 4-4. Nova Database Schema

Table Name	Description
migrate_version	Stores current version of the database schema as well as other migration-related info. Only used internally and by developers during upgrades.
migrations	Used for running host-to-host migration.
auth_tokens	Maps Authorization tokens (for all API transactions) to actual users (via the user id field).
certificates	Mappings for user, projects, and x509 certificates files
networks	Information pertaining to networks defined in Nova. Includes IP addressing, VLAN, and VPN information.
compute_nodes	Capabilities (vcpus, memory, etc.) and state (vcpus used, memory used, etc.) of each compute node.
projects	Information about projects, including project manager.

Table Name	Description
console_pools	Pool of consoles on the same physical node.
quotas	Quota overrides for particular projects. This is discussed further in "Quotas" on page 63.
consoles	Console session for an instance.
export_devices	Shelf and blade information used primarily with the AoE volume driver.
security_group_rules, security_groups and security_group_instance_association	Represent security groups and their associated rules.
fixed_ips and floating_ips	Associates the fixed and floating IP addresses to instances.
services	Listing off registered services (*nova-scheduler*, *nova-compute* and so on) and their current state. The updated_at field is used to determine if a given service is considered healthy or not.
instance_actions	Lists guest VM's actions and results.
user_project_association, user_project_role_association and user_role_association	Maintains relationship among users, projects, and roles.
instance_metadata	Metadata key/value pairs for an instance that is used during instance startup.
instance_types	Specifications (vCPUs, RAM, etc.) of flavors or instances types that users can use in this cloud. Described in much greater detail in "Instance Types and Flavors" on page 65.
instances	Representation of virtual machine instances.
users	Representations of users.
iscsi_targets	Mapping of iSCSI targets, hosts, and volumes.
volumes	Representation of volumes in the cloud.
key_pairs	Public key pairs for SSH.
zones	Represents a child zone of this zone. Only used in advanced configurations.

Nova supports a wide range of databases, including popular open-source stalwarts like MySQL (*http://mysql.com/*) and PostgreSQL (*http://www.postgresql.org/*). For more information on choosing an appropriate database for Nova, see "Database" on page 34.

## CHAPTER 5

Obtaining Nova

Nova is distributed from several sources in many different packaging formats. As it is a relatively new project, it lacks the installation ease and universal portability of more established open source projects like Apache Web Server. As such, it is not easily installable on every operating system distribution without significant administrative configuration. In this chapter, we will help you decide which version of the OpenStack code base is best suited to your deployment needs and show you how to obtain that version in your preferred packaging.

Nova Versions and Packaging

As Nova is a fast-moving and relatively young project, we need to make some decisions about the codebase that we want to use. There are two major decisions here:

- What version do we want to use?
- What form of packaging do we want to use to deploy Nova?

To adequately answer these questions, you need to ask yourself two tough questions:

- How proficient am I with Python development, system administration, and Linux packaging?
- How much stability am I willing to sacrifice to get the latest features?

To answer the proficiency question, you will need to honestly examine your skills across not just programming, but also system administration. If you don't utilize the packaged versions of Nova, you will need to understand how Python applications are built and their dependent packages. If you want to use newer, non-production versions of the code, it is possible that you will run into bugs that you will need to troubleshoot or fix yourself. On the systems administration side, Nova has heavy dependencies of Linux networking and virtualization support. As stated earlier in the book, it is mostly a control framework for virtual machines, storage, and networks. To apply its advanced configurations or options, you will need to understand the trade-offs you will be making. Rules of thumb for classifying skill level could be as follows:

Basic

Relatively unskilled in Python programming, but has basic system administration skills in Linux virtualization (specifically KVM) and networking (understanding of *iptables* and *ifconfig*).

Proficient

Beginner skills in Python (can read code, perhaps written basic Python scripts). Competent system administration skills, with advanced knowledge of key areas such as virtualization (perhaps deployed Xen or VMware at their company), storage (usage of iSCSI), and networking (understanding of VLANS and advanced switching).

Expert

Well-versed in Python, including working with large open-source Python projects, knowledge of popular libraries (SQL-Alchemy, amqplib, etc.), and experience with WSGI applications. Advanced system administration skills such as writing libvirt templates, defining new *iptables* or *ebtables* rules, and administering message queuing software.

As noted earlier in the book, Nova is a rapidly moving project that changes daily. Having said that, there are still regular releases, as with any normal software project. For the purposes of this book, we will look at three possible code releases that you might want to deploy:

Release

This is the last "released" version of the codebase and is analogous to a product release. Released versions of the code are the most tested and polished versions of OS. Release versions are suitable for production environments. Releases are referred to by their version number or their release name. For example, "2011.2" or "Cactus" was the third release of Nova.

Milestone

Between release versions, milestone versions are produced. These let leading-edge users familiarize themselves and test upcoming releases. Milestones are usually fairly stable, but probably only suitable for test and development environments. Milestones are referred to by the name of the upcoming release and the milestone number (such as "Diablo-3").

Trunk

Trunk refers to the most current version of the source code. After every update to the official Nova codebase (called a "commit") from any developer on the project, trunk is updated. This is the most volatile, least-tested, but most up-to-date release of the code. On many workdays, the trunk will get updated multiple times. Trunk is only recommended for users who are actively developing Nova. Trunk versions of the code are referred to by their Launchpad commit revision number (or "revno").

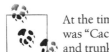 At the time of this writing (July 6th, 2011), the release version of Nova was "Cactus," or 2011.2; "Diablo-3" was the current milestone version; and trunk was at revno 1245.

Table 5-1 provides some guidance on which version and packaging format you'll be most successful at deploying depending on your proficiency and desired environment.

Table 5-1. Choosing Your Nova Version and Packaging

	Production	**Proof of Concept / Test**	**Development**
Basic	Product (Release-based)	N/A	N/A
Proficient	Package (Release-based)	Package (Milestone-based)	N/A
Expert	Source (Release-based)	Source (Milestone-based)	Source (Trunk-based)

Several of the cells within this table have been labelled "N/A" to indicate that these choices are not advised for the complexity of installation and skill level of the installer.

Distributions

Several companies are providing Nova as the basis of their distributions. For most people, this would be the equivalent of choosing Ubuntu or Red Hat Linux distributions instead of compiling their own Linux kernels. Distributions can provide installers, custom documentation, tested configurations, and support. For most people, distributions provide the quickest and easiest path from bare metal servers to working Nova deployments.

StackOps

StackOps offers "a complete, ready-to-use OpenStack distribution verified, tested and designed to reach as many users as possible thanks to a new and simple installation process." It is produced by a company of the same name.

The StackOps Distro installs on bare metal* (or virtual machine) via CD or USB drive and is based on a Ubuntu Linux Server 10.04 LTS. It features a "Smart Installer" that creates deployments with default settings in three different modes: single node, dual node, and multi node. The installer will also let you add more nodes to an existing installation.

With a focus on ease of installation and excellent documentation, this is an ideal choice for those looking to evaluate or test Nova. You can download or learn more about this distribution at *http://www.stackops.com/*.

---

* In this instance "bare metal" refers to a server without an operating system already installed.

Later in this book, we use StackOps to install and configure a single-system Nova deployment.

Citrix "Project Olympus"

Citrix has created "Project Olympus," which aims to provide a "tested, certified and supported version of OpenStack" along with a "cloud-optimized version of XenServer." While this is not yet a released project, you can learn more details and sign up for the early access program at *http://deliver.citrix.com/projectolympus*. It is slated for general availability later in 2011.

Nova Packages

For most competent system administrators, package installation is the preferred method of software installation. Like products or distributions, packages provide for easy and quick installations. However, unlike distributions, package installations tend to require more individual pieces (and dependencies) and do not provide assistance with configuration. On the other hand, they do provide more flexibility in that the administrator can pick and choose the pieces they would like to install. The sections below outline the methods to obtain packages for many of today's popular server operating systems.

Launchpad Ubuntu Packages

The source of all Nova packages is the code repository at Launchpad. If you want to closely follow the codebase, you should configure your system to obtain its packages from the PPA repositories at Launchpad.

 Personal Package Archives (PPAs) is a Launchpad feature that builds Ubuntu packages from a user's hosted source code and then distributes them to the public. OpenStack has taken advantage of this automated feature to produce several different repositories of Nova packages, each containing different snapshots of Nova code. We'll talk about the Nova PPAs later, but you can learn more about creating your own PPAs at *https://help.launchpad.net/Packaging/PPA*.

Release

If you want to run the latest release of Nova (2011.2 or "Cactus") on Ubuntu, you can use the personal project archives (PPA) at Launchpad. You can enable packages from the PPAs by executing the following commands:

```
$ sudo apt-get install python-software-properties
$ sudo add-apt-repository ppa:openstack-release/2011.2
$ sudo apt-get update
```

Replace the *2011.2* part of the add-apt-repository command above with any other OpenStack release designation to use that release. For example, you can access the "Bexar" packages with the *sudo add-apt-repository ppa:openstack-release/2011.1* command.

These releases are production quality.

Milestone

You can install slightly newer (which might provide additional functionality and bugs) by using development milestones that are released approximately every four weeks. You can enable those PPAs with the following commands:

```
$ sudo apt-get install python-software-properties
$ sudo add-apt-repository ppa:nova-core/milestone
$ sudo apt-get update
```

You can access the current development milestone schedule on the OpenStack Wiki (*http://wiki.openstack.org/*). For example, the current "Diablo" milestone schedule is located at *http://wiki.openstack.org/DiabloReleaseSchedule*.

These packages are not production quality. They should be used for testing and development.

Trunk

Just as you can get the last release or milestone packages, you can also get the latest trunk code as packages. This is the same command-line process as the release or milestone packages but specifies the trunk repository:

```
$ sudo apt-get install python-software-properties
$ sudo add-apt-repository ppa:nova-core/trunk
$ sudo apt-get update
```

As stated earlier in this chapter, trunk changes very rapidly and is the least stable of all the packages. It is prudent to review current bug reports on Launchpad before upgrading your packages on trunk, unless you're actively trying to reproduce bugs.

These packages are not production quality and should only be used for development.

Ubuntu Distribution Packages

Ubuntu recently made the decision to include OpenStack (Nova, Glance, and Swift) as part of the official Ubuntu 11.04 "Natty" release. These packages are the latest release

(2011.2 "Cactus") at the time of Ubuntu 11.04 debut. You'll find these packages in the Ubuntu universe repository. They can be installed just like the Launchpad packages.

Red Hat Enterprise Linux Packages

A consulting company named Grid Dynamics (*http://www.griddynamics.com/*) provides Nova and Glance RPM packages for Red Hat Enterprise Linux. However, there are some differences between these packages and the Ubuntu versions. These are summarized as:

- The packages use libguestfs instead of NBD (*http://www.xss.co.at/linux/NBD/*) for qcow2 image support.
- Network injection code (configuration of the instances' networking) was patched for a new path (*/etc/sysconfig/network-scripts*) and template.
- Only KVM hypervisor has been tested.

Complete instructions and links to the development repositories can be found via the RHEL Packaging page (*http://wiki.openstack.org/Packaging/RHEL*) on the OpenStack wiki or by going to their build page directly at *http://yum.griddynamics.net/*.

Fedora Packages

Another consulting company called Mirantis (*http://mirantis.com/*) provides Nova Fedora packages based on the Red Hat Enterprise Linux packages. They provide both Cactus release and trunk packages.

Instructions for installing these RPMs and configuring them with a kickstart script are available at the Mirantis blog (*http://mirantis.blogspot.com/2011/05/openstack-deploy ment-on-fedora-using.html*).

Microsoft Windows

It is unlikely that you will be able to fully install Nova on Microsoft Windows. Microsoft Windows lacks many of the Nova-supporting Python libraries and is not supported by Nova orchestration features (which are mostly Linux operating system commands). While Microsoft Windows is not suitable for the core Nova daemons, Microsoft Hyper-V (*http://www.microsoft.com/hyper-v-server/en/us/default.aspx*) is supported as a compute host.

For more information on using Hyper-V as a virtualization technology on your compute hosts, be sure to consult the Hyper-V development wiki page (*http://wiki.openstack.org/ HypervInstall*).

Source Code

Source code gives you access to the rawest, most flexible, and most up-to-date versions of Nova. However, that flexibility requires the most proficiency on the part of the end user to install, configure, and deploy. To gather Nova in source code format, you will need a few special tools, some knowledge of Python development, and a bit of patience.

The Nova source code can either be downloaded as a compressed tarball or via the bazaar source control system. Unless you already happen to develop with bazaar, it is easier to just download as the tarball. All the releases are available at *https://launchpad.net/nova/+download*. Instructions for installing from source are available on the OpenStack wiki "Install From Source" article (*http://wiki.openstack.org/InstallFromSource*).

## CHAPTER 6

Planning Nova Deployment

As Nova supports a wide range of technologies, configurations, and designs, it will be important to make a number of architectural and design decisions before looking to deploy it. This section guides you through the most important ones before you begin.

Deployment of Nova can be painless with good planning. However, Nova does have a lot of moving parts, so it's good to understand an overview of what is trying to be accomplished before you start installing software. Figure 6-1 illustrates the preferred workflow for installing, configuring, and launching your first instance on Nova.

This is a three-step process:

- Planning Nova Deployment to decide on deployment scenario, finalize key design choices, and ensure hardware meets requirements
- Installing Nova to get the software, prerequisites, and configurations onto the servers
- Using Nova to prep the system for your initial users

 This book covers the infrastructure for clouds. As such, it is out of scope of the book to describe everything that you will want to do with your cloud instance once you have it running.

At each phase of the installation, we will make sure to test the results of our actions. Without these tests, it is very easy to get to the last steps and find out you need to start over again due to error in an early phase.

Virtualization Technology

As you can see from the earlier discussion of Nova's architecture, there are ample choices for virtualization products. I will not go into all the factors about the appro-

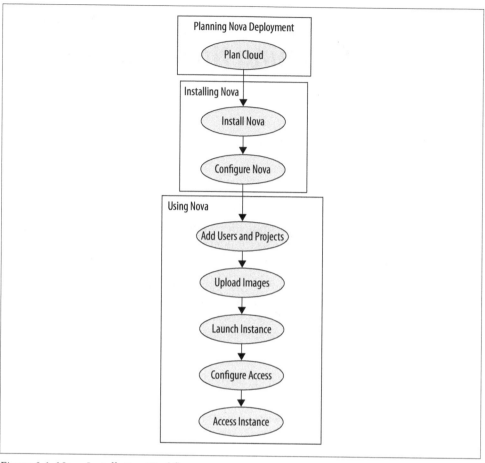

Figure 6-1. Nova Installation Workflow

priate virtualization technology to choose here, but if you have an installed base of hypervisors, that will need to be factored into your cloud platform choice.

 Nova requires all compute hosts within a zone to use a single virtualization technology. For example, you cannot mix VMware-based compute hosts with KVM-based compute hosts. They will all need to be one or the other. This may change in future releases.

Unless you already have extensive experience with particular virtualization technology, most people will gravitate toward either KVM or a Xen-based solution (Xen/XCP/Xen-Server). Each has its own advantages:

- KVM ships with most operating systems and is easy to install and configure. It has arguably the best support within Nova (supporting advanced Nova features like live migration) and is easy to get support on, as it is used widely in the community.

However, many people feel that it has greater overhead (especially in I/O) and doesn't support some high-end virtualization like memory ballooning.

- Xen-based solutions, on the other hand, excel at performance and have been used in some of the largest clouds in the world. It is rumored to power Rackspace's compute cloud, Amazon's EC2, and GoGrid's cloud. However, this comes at the price of complexity, as they are much more challenging to install, configure, and maintain for people inexperienced with enterprise virtualization products.

The general rule of thumb at the current time is to configure KVM for small or non-production deployments but use a Xen-based technology for large-scale production installations.

Authentication

Nova can authenticate against a number of sources. By default, it will use the local configuration database (the one specified by the `--sql_connection` flag) for this. However, the current version of Nova also supports LDAP for authentication. LDAP authentication requires significantly more setup. Setup help is available for OpenSSH, OpenLDAP, Sun's LDAP, and OpenDJ. For more information about setting up these options, consult the *nova/auth/* directory in the Nova source.

API

Nova features a pluggable architecture for API support. The current Nova incarnation supports:

- OpenStack API 1.0 (with preliminary OpenStack 1.1 API support)
- Amazon EC2 API

Many customers will probably request the mostly compatible EC2 API interface, which supports about 90% of Amazon's current implementation. However, the OpenStack API (especially the 1.1 version) will probably be the more widely implemented version in the long run, as it is an open API not controlled by a single company.

While there is no technical requirement to pick one API over the other, it will be confusing to your users if they need to use both. Very few users tools or libraries will support both and allow them to switch on an API by API call basis.

Scheduler

There are many choices for your scheduler. As stated earlier, this is a conceptually simple, but vitally important part of your deployment. The scheduler places instances (virtual servers) onto specific compute hosts. While this may not be vitally important if you only have one or two compute nodes, it is absolutely critical once you start to grow. Most installations will start with the `simple` scheduler and then write their own scheduler as they grow. If writing your own scheduler is not feasible for your installation, the next version of Nova ("Diablo") will feature more choices.

Image Service

Images can be a management headache for many installations. While using Glance along with Swift is the clear choice for larger installations, its management overhead and additional configuration complexity may be too much for smaller deployments. In these cases, *nova-objectstore* is probably the best alternative.

Even if you choose Glance as your image catalog, you may still need the *nova-objectstore* on your machine. For emulation of the Amazon EC2 AMI uploading and bundling semantics, Nova uses the *nova-objectstore* as a temporary holding space for various pieces of the AMI. Only once all the pieces have arrived are they assembled and transported into Glance.

Database

As stated earlier, Nova uses a Python library called SQL-Alchemy (*http://www.sqlalchemy.org/*) for database abstraction and access. As such, Nova can theoretically support any database product that SQL-Alchemy supports. However, in practice, there are only three with any level of testing and support within the Nova community:

sqlite3
> While sqlite3 is the default database for development and testing, it is unsuitable for production installation due to scalability, availability, and performance concerns.

MySQL
> MySQL is far and away the most popular database for Nova production deployments. It is also arguably easiest to setup with Nova, and almost all of the documentation assumes you are using it. It should be the default choice for most users.

PostgreSQL
> PostgreSQL is a distant third in usage within the Nova community. However, there is a dedicated group using it and it does possess many advantageous features for use in large-scale production sites. Users with strong experience in deploying and tuning PostgreSQL may find this an attractive option.

Assuming that you are looking for a production deployment, the decision for database product should come down to PostgreSQL or MySQL. Unless you have significant experience with PostgreSQL, MySQL will be a better choice, as all documentation is written with MySQL in mind and there is a larger support community.

Volumes

Volume storage design should be treated with particular care, as it is one of the few components of Nova that stores non-ephemeral data. Most large installations will look at using either the SAN or iSCSI options for this, as it allows them to utilize enterprise-class hardware and software for greater availability and redundancy. However, specialized installations (especially high-performance computing or research) may try the less production-ready drivers (RDB or Sheepdog) if their data survivability is not paramount.

Installing Nova

With the basics and theory behind us, it is time to get hands-on with Nova and install the code on a server. In this chapter, we will walk through the installation and configuration of Nova on a single node with both the StackOps distro and Ubuntu packages. You'll get a feeling for the complexities of implementing your design choices in actual usage. While these installations will be only single nodes, they will contain the entire array of OpenStack software and features.

Installing Nova with StackOps

As we described back in "StackOps" on page 25, StackOps provides a distro for Open-Stack with a bare metal installer. The bare metal installer automates most of the installation and configuration tasks, leaving very little command line or configuration file editing for the administrator. It will install an operating system, necessary software packages, and Nova configuration files for us.

 Installing StackOps will overwrite any operating system on your server. It is not intended to overlay Nova onto already installed servers.

Since our purpose is to get some hands-on experience with Nova, we will be installing a single node that runs all the services. As StackOps is a full distribution, it makes many of the cloud design choices for us. The single node installation has made the following design choices:

- *nova-api* supporting both the OpenStack API and EC2 API
- *nova-objectstore* (instead of Glance) for an image service
- *nova-volume* with iSCSI volumes
- *nova-network* using FlatDHCP manager (configurable)
- MySQL for our database

- RabbitMQ for the messaging queue
- *nova-compute* using KVM or UML for virtualization
- MySQL database for authentication
- *nova-scheduler* chance (default) scheduler

If you have any problems following along with the installation, you can find more detailed documentation at the StackOps Documentation Site (*http://docs.stackops .org/*).

Check StackOps Requirements

StackOps has a very basic set of requirements for a minimal installation as you can see in Table 7-1. While these minimal requirements will get the system installed and running, you will be constrained in the number of virtual machines that you can launch. At the base 2GB of RAM, you might only be able to launch a single small instance.

Table 7-1. Minimal StackOps Configuration

Component	Specification
CPU	Intel or AMD x64
RAM	2GB
Disk	1 x 30GB Drive
NIC	1 x 1GbE

As you can see, this minimal configuration should be able to be satisfied by most desktops or servers bought within the last few years.

Of course, the minimal requirements are only useful for a proof of concept or experimental system, but it fits perfectly for our needs. A more appropriately configured system could be used as a production system. The baseline for this would be as shown in Table 7-2.

Table 7-2. Baseline StackOps Configuration

Component	Specification
CPU	2 x Intel/AMD x64
RAM	32GB
Disk	2 x 2TB SATA RAID 1 Drives
	2 x 32GB SAS/SSD/SATA RAID 1 Drives
NIC	2 x 1GbE

For the purposes of this book, we will be installing on a very small server system called an HP ProLiant MicroServer™. While the exact model is irrelevant, it does show that

StackOps and Nova can be installed on relatively inexpensive and modestly configured hardware (The MicroServer retails for under $400 in the United States). The test server specifications are shown in Table 7-3.

Table 7-3. StackOps Test Server Specifications

Component	Specification
CPU	AMD Athlon II Neo 36L Dual Core (64 Bit CPU running at 1.4 Mhz)
RAM	4GB
Disk	1 x 250GB SATA Drive
NIC	2 x 1GBE

Download StackOps

The StackOps Distro is available free from their community website at *http://www .stackops.org/*. It comes in several versions and two formats (CD or USB stick image). For the purposes of this book, we will be using version `0.2.1 - Build 112 (stack ops-0.2.1-b112-d20110517)`, which is based on the Nova "Cactus" release. Once you have downloaded the software, burn it to a CD or transfer it to your USB stick (depending on which image you downloaded).

Install StackOps

Now that we have our CD or USB stick ready, we will go ahead and install it on our server. As we decided earlier, we will be installing a single node system (everything running on one server) with basic network and iSCSI volumes. StackOps makes most of these configuration decisions easy for us with their predefined deployment scenarios. All together, they offer four deployment scenarios:

- Single Node: All in one deployment.
- Dual Node: One cloud controller node (everything but *nova-compute*) and one compute node. This is the smallest viable production configuration.
- Multi-Node: A four node plus configuration with dedicated *nova-network*, *nova-compute*, and *nova-volume* nodes. This is a fairly advanced configuration that requires specialized networking.
- Advanced Multi-Node: An upcoming configuration that adds monitoring and other options to create a larger scale production installation.

We'll use the "Single Node" scenario for this exercise.

Install Operating System

Your first step in installing your StackOps distro is the installation of the operation system, all the necessary prerequisite packages, OpenStack packages, and preconfigured nova components. In addition, it installs an agent that configures OpenStack for you. When you first boot your system with the CD or USB Stick, you'll be greeted with the StackOps splash screen (as seen in Figure 7-1) that resembles most Linux distro installations.

Figure 7-1. StackOps Installation Screen

After choosing the "Install StackOps Controller Node," you'll be led through a number of standard Linux installation screens. They will ask you about your language and keyboard layout before installing a number of basic components.

After it has completed the basic components installation, it will ask you to configure your network settings. Enter your IP address, management network IP, netmask, and default gateway address. It will then try and contact a public NTP (Network Time Protocol) server. If it fails, it will ask you to specify one manually.

 StackOps requires that the nodes have static IP addresses, not DHCP provided ones.

Since I am putting this server on my home network, I have chosen 192.168.1.65 as my server node IP address. This is out of my home router's DHCP block so that I won't have any conflicts. I've set the gateway address to 192.168.1.254 (my DSL router) and used the normal 255.255.255.0 netmask.

Once the network has been configured, you will move on to disk partitioning. This shows standard Linux disk partitioning screens.

 To complete this installation and use *nova-volume*, you need to have one extra empty partition. This can be an extra hard drive in your machine, an external hard drive, or extra partition. If you only have only one hard drive (like the machine in this example), you should create an unused partition in this step. If you don't, you'll need an external hard drive to complete the install. In my example, I simply plugged a 16GB flash drive into the USB port.

After the disk is partitioned and formatted, the base operating system and OpenStack packages will be installed. This will take a while. When it is finished, pop out the CD or USB stick and reboot the machine. It should boot to the command prompt, as shown in Figure 7-2.

```
StackOps Openstack Distribution 0.2.1-b112-d20110517

To configure this node, connect to http://192.168.1.10:8888

nova-controller login: _
```

Figure 7-2. StackOps Login Screen

Now that the machine is up and running, let's test to make sure everything went all right before we move on to configuring our cloud. Login to the server as the "root" user with the password "stackops" to get a root user prompt. Check to make sure that the StackOps agent is running by checking its log file:

```
# more /var/log/nova/installer-agent.py.log
2011-07-04 11:28:14-0700 [-] Log opened.
2011-07-04 11:28:14-0700 [-] Starting server: 2011-07-04 11:28:14.515648
2011-07-04 11:28:14-0700 [-] twisted.web.server.Site starting on 8888
```

Configure with Smart Installer

With the basic distro successfully installed, it is now time to configure the Nova software. StackOps has an agent-based "Smart Installer" that guides you through the configuration process, gives you intelligent defaults, and then applies the configuration to your newly installed server. While we are only using it for a simple single-node install here, it will also configure and apply to multiple servers according to their role in the deployment scenario.

The first step in running the Smart Installer is to connect a web browser to the address shown in the banner of your server's login screen. This should be an address in the form of http://xxx.xxx.xxx.xxx:8888/, where xxx.xxx.xxx.xxx is your server's IP address. Once you connect to that address, you will be redirected to Smart Installer login screen.

> Your browser will need to have access to the Internet. It acts as a middleman between the two, gathering config data from your server and transferring to the configuration web application. Your server does not need access to the Internet.

The first screen of the Smart Installer will ask you to create an account and then login. While creating an account is not a necessity, it will allow you to save, edit, and redeploy your configurations later. Figure 7-3 shows the login screen.

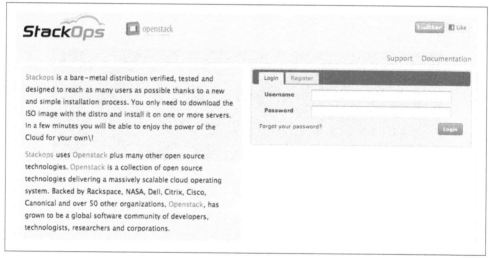

Figure 7-3. StackOps Smart Installer Login

Once registered and logged in, the Smart Installer will step you through a number of screens to configure your Nova deployment. The first screen is the most important: choosing your deployment scenario (Figure 7-4). We will be using the "single node" scenario.

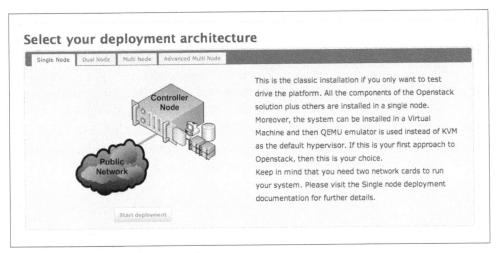

Figure 7-4. StackOps Deployment Architecture

Next, it will help you configure your controller functions (*nova-api*, networks, database, queue, etc.) of your installation. The first of these screens will review your hardware configuration, as shown in Figure 7-5.

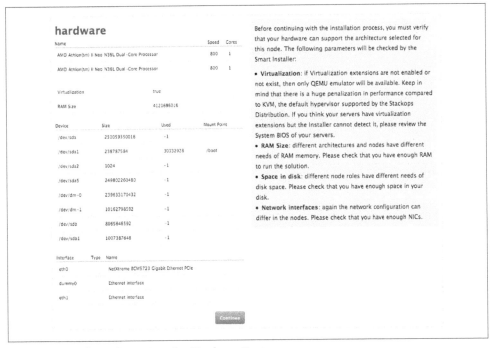

Figure 7-5. StackOps Smart Installer Hardware Review

Once you review the hardware configurations, you can advance to the software requirements screen. This is also a read-only screen, and after reviewing your server network configuration, you can go on to the next screen.

The next screen shows the configuration options for network topologies. Since we are using a single-interface test server, we don't need to change anything (it should be preset to your eth0 interface). In more advanced deployment scenarios, this screen lets you assign separate service, storage, and public networks. Advance to the next screen.

The next screen is the most important screen of our configuration. It shows the global service options. This screen allows you to customize the configurations for:

- Database
- Queue
- EC2 API
- S3 repository
- Authentication
- Logging
- Network

Of all these options, the only one that we **must** edit is the network section. Figure 7-6 shows the networking options.

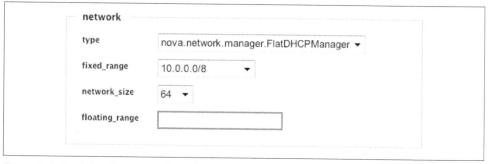

Figure 7-6. StackOps Smart Installer Global Networking

Pay close attention these configurations. Misconfiguring this step will result in your instances not starting or being unable to be reached. Use the following guidelines for these options:

- type: Choose your network manager. We will leave this at `nova.network.man ager.FlatDHCPManager`.
- fixed_range: Choose your fixed (private) IP address range. It is fine to use the default 10.0.0.0/8 range as long as this does not conflict with your current network settings. As I use the 192.168.1.0/24 range on my internal network, I will leave the default.

- network size: Choose the size of your fixed IP range. For this single node installation, this is not relevant, but we will make it smaller. My test server uses 8.
- floating range: This is the most important entry. Enter the range for your floating IPs (public addresses) that are available on your network. Since my internal network uses the 192.168.1.0/24 range, I have configured my router to only give out IP addresses in the 192.168.1.1 - 192.168.1.64 range. I decided to have my instances use the addresses in the 192.168.1.129 - 192.168.1.134 range. Consulting my handy subnet calculator, I used `192.168.1.128/29` for this entry.

 This is the most likely place that your installation will go wrong. Make sure that you carefully plan and review your entries here. If you are in doubt, consult your local network administrator.

When you are satisfied with your network options, move on to the compute screen. All the options on this screen should be fine for our test installation. The only option that you might want to review is your `libvirt type`. This pull-down menu lets you choose between QEMU and KVM virtualization. Unless you do not have a KVM capable machine, you should leave it on KVM.

The final configuration screen for the Smart Installer is the volume options. You may need to change the `lvm_device` option to the device path for your empty partition that you created during the "Install Operating System" on page 39 step.

 As the screen says, "Choose a device that you are 100% sure is not already in use!" This device will be completely erased. I usually use a blank USB stick for this step and choose /dev/sdb1 from the pull-down menu.

With the volume configuration done, you are ready to install your configuration to your server, as shown in Figure 7-7.

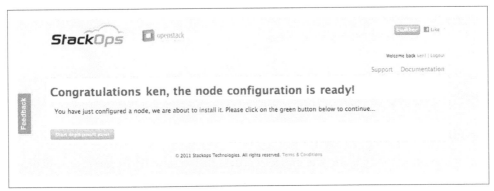

Figure 7-7. StackOps Smart Installer Ready To Install

Test StackOps Installation

Now that we have finished the installation and configuration, let's make sure that everything is up and running. Log in into your Nova server as root with the 'stackops' password. Once you've logged into the server, add the Nova binaries to your path.

```
# export PATH=$PATH:/var/lib/nova/bin/
```

Then check to make sure all the services are up and running with the *nova-manage* command.

```
# nova-manage service list
nova-controller nova-compute   enabled  :-) 2011-07-07 06:53:05
nova-controller nova-network   enabled  :-) 2011-07-07 06:52:58
nova-controller nova-scheduler enabled  :-) 2011-07-07 06:53:04
nova-controller nova-volume    enabled  :-) 2011-07-07 06:53:04
```

As you can see, we've used the *nova-manage* command with the `service list` arguments to query the database and see which services are registered, enabled, and running. The "smiley" field (the `:-)` between the 'enabled' and last checked in fields) shows that each of the services are healthy. If they hadn't checked in with the database in a while, we would see 'XXX' in their listing. The *nova-manage* command is covered more thoroughly in Chapter 9.

Installing Nova from Packages

For this installation, we will use a slightly more powerful machine. This machine is a workstation-class machine with more RAM and a faster processor. Please note that we don't need any more powerful a machine for this installation—I simply would like to run more virtual instances. We could use the exact same machine as in the StackOps installation section.

Table 7-4. Packages Test Server Specifications

Component	Specification
CPU	AMD Phenom™ 9550 Quad-Core Processor
RAM	8GB
Disk	1 x 1TB SATA Drive
NIC	2 x 1GBE

Install Base Operating System

We will assume that we are starting with a default Ubuntu 10.10 server installation. The only software packages that we have installed beyond the basics are the "virtual machine host" and "openssh server" options. Just as with the StackOps installation, we have installed the server with fixed IP addresses and an empty partition for use with *nova-volume*.

Install Nova Packages

Install Prerequisites

Now that we are sure that virtualization works on our single machine, let's complete a few more dependencies for Nova. Install RabbitMQ as our message queue by adding the *rabbitmq-server* package.

 Before installing RabbitMQ, make sure that your hostname is set to your correct IP address in your */etc/hosts* file. Without this correctly entered, RabbitMQ will refuse to start.

```
$ sudo apt-get install rabbitmq-server
```

This will drag along a number of packages with it, mainly erlang ones. You can check to make sure this is running with the *rabbitmqctl*:

```
$ sudo rabbitmqctl status
Status of node rabbit@cactus ...
[{running_applications,[{rabbit,"RabbitMQ","1.8.0"},
                        {mnesia,"MNESIA  CXC 138 12","4.4.12"},
                        {os_mon,"CPO  CXC 138 46","2.2.4"},
                        {sasl,"SASL  CXC 138 11","2.1.8"},
                        {stdlib,"ERTS  CXC 138 10","1.16.4"},
                        {kernel,"ERTS  CXC 138 10","2.13.4"}]},
 {nodes,[rabbit@cactus]},
 {running_nodes,[rabbit@cactus]}]
...done.
```

Install MySQL as your database with the *mysql-server* package if it is not already installed on your server:

```
$ sudo apt-get install mysql-server
```

When it asks for your MySQL password, remember to write down the password, as we will need it later. With the database server installed, let's create the Nova database.

 If you are going to use this database with machines other than just this one, you need to edit your */etc/mysql/my.cnf* configuration file. Specifically, you need to change the `bind-address = 127.0.0.1` to `bind-address = 0.0.0.0` so that it listens on all your network interfaces, not just the loopback.

```
$ mysqladmin -u root -p create nova
$ mysqlshow -u root -p
Enter password:
+--------------------+
|     Databases      |
+--------------------+
| information_schema |
```

```
| mysql              |
| nova               |
+--------------------+
```

With the database created, we now need to make an account for the user nova. We'll just use some quick SQL statements to grant privileges and set the password before we login to make sure we did it correctly.

```
$ mysql -u root -p  -e "GRANT ALL PRIVILEGES ON *.* TO 'nova'@'%' WITH GRANT OPTION;"
Enter password:
$ mysql -uroot -p -e "SET PASSWORD FOR 'nova'@'%' = PASSWORD('nova');"
Enter password:
$ mysql -u nova -p nova
Enter password:
Welcome to the MySQL monitor.  Commands end with ; or \g.
Your MySQL connection id is 56
Server version: 5.1.49-1ubuntu8.1 (Ubuntu)

Copyright (c) 2000, 2010, Oracle and/or its affiliates. All rights reserved.
This software comes with ABSOLUTELY nova-objectstore WARRANTY. This is free software,
and you are welcome to modify and redistribute it under the GPL v2 license

Type 'help;' or '\h' for help. Type '\c' to clear the current input statement.

mysql>
```

Finally, add a few final prerequisite packages for this specific configuration:

```
$ sudo apt-get install python-greenlet python-mysqldb python-software-properties dnsmasq
```

The first three are necessary Python libraries and the last one will give us DHCP and other services for *nova-network*.

The final prerequisite is installing and configuring iSCSI for *nova-volume*. This is a two-step process: creating the volume group with Linux Volume Manager (LVM) and starting iSCSI services. To create the volume group, use the following commands (we are using */dev/sde1* for this simple example):

```
$ sudo pvcreate /dev/sde1
  Physical volume "/dev/sde1" successfully created
$ sudo vgcreate nova-volumes /dev/sde1
  Volume group "nova-volumes" successfully created
```

 Your volume group needs to be called nova-volume for *nova-volume* to recognize it. Volumes will not work with another volume group name.

To start iSCSI services, simply make sure that the ISCSITARGET_ENABLE option is set to true in the */etc/default/iscsitarget* file and start the *iscsitarget* service:

```
$ sudo sed -i 's/false/true/g' /etc/default/iscsitarget
$ sudo service iscsitarget start
```

With these final steps complete, we are done with installing and configuring the Nova prerequisites.

Install Nova

Now let's make sure we've added the Launchpad PPAs to our configuration:

```
$ sudo add-apt-repository ppa:openstack-release/2011.2
Executing: gpg --ignore-time-conflict --no-options --no-default-keyring
--secret-keyring /etc/apt/secring.gpg --trustdb-name /etc/apt/trustdb.gpg
--keyring /etc/apt/trusted.gpg --primary-keyring /etc/apt/trusted.gpg
--keyserver keyserver.ubuntu.com --recv 94CA80414F1043F6495425C37D21C2EC3D1B4472
gpg: requesting key 3D1B4472 from hkp server keyserver.ubuntu.com
gpg: key 3D1B4472: public key "Launchpad PPA for OpenStack release team" imported
gpg: Total number processed: 1
gpg:               imported: 1  (RSA: 1)
$ sudo apt-get update
```

Now let's move onto installing the Nova packages, which will drag a few more dependencies with it. Type the following command:

```
$ sudo apt-get install -y nova-common nova-doc nova-api \
    nova-network nova-objectstore nova-scheduler nova-compute \
    python-nova nova-volume unzip
```

These install lines added most of the packages that you would expect (*nova-api*, *nova-compute*, etc.), along with a large number of dependencies. In addition, the package installation scripts have added a system user "nova" and added it to the appropriate groups.

It has also set up a minimal configuration file in */etc/nova/nova.conf* for you:

```
$ more /etc/nova/nova.conf
--dhcpbridge_flagfile=/etc/nova/nova.conf
--dhcpbridge=/usr/bin/nova-dhcpbridge
--logdir=/var/log/nova
--state_path=/var/lib/nova
--lock_path=/var/lock/nova
--verbose
```

Now let's make sure that Nova sees all of our services and they are running:

```
$ sudo nova-manage service list
cactus      nova-network enabled   :-) 2011-07-10 00:04:39.928905
cactus      nova-compute enabled   :-) 2011-07-10 00:04:40.154642
cactus      nova-scheduler enabled  :-) 2011-07-10 00:04:40.044152
cactus      nova-volume enabled   :-) 2011-07-10 00:04:43.540773
```

 Chapter 9 explains the use of *nova-manage* in much greater detail.

Since we are seeing all smiley faces, it looks like Nova is installed correctly.

Install Glance

Now that we have Nova on the server, let's install Glance as our image service:

```
$ sudo apt-get install glance python-glance-doc
```

This installation will use the default configuration, which uses sqlite3 for the database.

Configure OpenStack

First, let's configure it to use our MySQL database that we created earlier. To do this, just add the following flag to the */etc/nova.conf* config file:

```
--sql_connection=mysql://nova:nova@127.0.0.1/nova
```

This flag contains the driver ("mysql:"), user and password separated by a colon ("nova:nova"), the server address or hostname ("127.0.0.1"), and the database name ("/nova"). It also optionally includes the mysql port number after the hostname or server IP address.

We will also set our installation to use KVM for virtualization. While this is the default, it is a good practice to explicitly set it in the */etc/nova.conf* file.

```
--libvirt_type=kvm
```

Now let's set Nova to use the Glance installation by adding these two options to */etc/nova.conf*:

```
--glance_host=127.0.0.1
--image_service=nova.image.glance.GlanceImageService
```

With that completed, we'll move on to configuring the networking options. First up is adding the network manager related options to */etc/nova.conf*:

```
--network_manager=nova.network.manager.FlatDHCPManager
--fixed_range=10.0.0.0/8
--network_size=8
```

Now, let's add our network into the database with the *nova-manage* command:

```
# nova-manage network create 10.0.0.0/8 1 8
```

Finally, we will create the floating addresses using a range that will not overlap with the StackOps installation.

```
# nova-manage floating create cactus 192.168.1.136/29
```

With all the */etc/nova.conf* changes made, we can create the database schema by running the *nova-manage db* commands. First, we will *sync* the database (create the schema), then we will *version* the database to make sure that the schema creation succeeded.

```
$ sudo nova-manage db sync
$ sudo nova-manage db version
14
```

And we are done with the configuration. All that is left to do now is restart the Nova daemons to pick the new configuration options.

```
$ sudo restart libvirt-bin; sudo restart nova-network; sudo restart nova-compute; \
  sudo restart nova-api; sudo restart nova-objectstore; sudo restart nova-scheduler; \
  sudo restart nova-volume
libvirt-bin start/running, process 22673
nova-network start/running, process 22729
nova-compute start/running, process 22776
nova-api start/running, process 22838
nova-objectstore start/running, process 22846
nova-scheduler start/running, process 22933
```

## CHAPTER 8

Using Nova

Now that we have a working Nova installation, we need to ready it for use by our initial users. This requires us to do some command-line configuration on the Nova controller (or the server with the database). First, we will add a user, then upload a virtual disk image, launch the instance, and finally configure network access for it.

Creating User and Projects

The first step is using our new Nova installation is to create a user. This is a multi-step process that uses the *nova-manage* utility to create a project.

```
# nova-manage user create ken
export EC2_ACCESS_KEY=d77406c3-cea1-45af-bbd9-acfd16ff49e3
export EC2_SECRET_KEY=b9c6ab50-65d7-4185-a1a9-267a2afe30f9
# nova-manage role add ken cloudadmin
# nova-manage project create book ken
# nova-manage project zipfile book ken
```

The final command in the example will produce a zip-compressed file called *nova.zip*. Now uncompress the credential zip file and source the resulting *novarc*. This will set a number of environmental variables needed to access your Nova installation with other utilities. If you are creating this user on behalf of another user, you will need to give him this zipfile.

```
# unzip nova.zip
Archive:  nova.zip
 extracting: novarc
 extracting: pk.pem
 extracting: cert.pem
 extracting: cacert.pem
# . ./novarc
```

While not necessary, you might want to view *novarc* to find out what environmental variables it is setting for you. Remember that you will need to source this file in every session if you want to access your Nova deployment. You might want to add it to your shell profile to have it automatically sourced on login.

```
# more novarc
NOVA_KEY_DIR=$(pushd $(dirname $BASH_SOURCE)>/dev/null; pwd; popd>/dev/null)
export EC2_ACCESS_KEY="d77406c3-cea1-45af-bbd9-acfd16ff49e3:book"
export EC2_SECRET_KEY="b9c6ab50-65d7-4185-a1a9-267a2afe30f9"
export EC2_URL="http://192.168.1.65:8773/services/Cloud"
export S3_URL="http://192.168.1.65:3333"
export EC2_USER_ID=42 # nova does not use user id, but bundling requires it
export EC2_PRIVATE_KEY=${NOVA_KEY_DIR}/pk.pem
export EC2_CERT=${NOVA_KEY_DIR}/cert.pem
export NOVA_CERT=${NOVA_KEY_DIR}/cacert.pem
export EUCALYPTUS_CERT=${NOVA_CERT} \
# euca-bundle-image seems to require this set
alias ec2-bundle-image="ec2-bundle-image --cert ${EC2_CERT} --privatekey \
${EC2_PRIVATE_KEY} --user 42 --ec2cert ${NOVA_CERT}"
alias ec2-upload-bundle="ec2-upload-bundle -a ${EC2_ACCESS_KEY} \
-s ${EC2_SECRET_KEY} --url ${S3_URL} --ec2cert ${NOVA_CERT}"
export NOVA_API_KEY="d77406c3-cea1-45af-bbd9-acfd16ff49e3"
export NOVA_USERNAME="ken"
export NOVA_URL="http://192.168.1.65:8774/v1.0/"
```

Uploading Images

Before we can launch instances, we need to upload a virtual disk image into Nova. There are a number of different images that you can use with your Nova installation. You can also make your own images.

For the purposes of our test server setup, let's use Ubuntu's Enterprise Cloud images. We'll download the newest Ubuntu Server image for use on our cloud.

```
# wget \
>http://uec-images.ubuntu.com/server/releases/natty/release/\
>ubuntu-11.04-server-uec-amd64.tar.gz
```

Once we have that image, we need to upload it into the Nova image store. How we do this varies depending on the image store that we've chosen. For our StackOps installation (which uses the *nova-objectstore*), we can use the *uec-publish-tarball* utility. To use this utility, give it the compressed image and container/bucket name (I've used *images* as my bucket name for this example).

```
# uec-publish-tarball ubuntu-11.04-server-uec-amd64.tar.gz images
Mon Jul  4 13:25:19 PDT 2011: ====== extracting image ======
Warning: no ramdisk found, assuming '--ramdisk none'
kernel : natty-server-uec-amd64-vmlinuz-virtual
ramdisk: none
image  : natty-server-uec-amd64.img
Mon Jul  4 13:25:32 PDT 2011: ====== bundle/upload kernel ======
Mon Jul  4 13:25:34 PDT 2011: ====== bundle/upload image ======
Mon Jul  4 13:26:46 PDT 2011: ====== done ======
emi="ami-6683ba18"; eri="none"; eki="aki-7eea4179";
```

The emi="ami-6683ba18" part is what we are interested in. It is the machine image. We'll use it later when we launch an instance.

Now that we have images, let's make sure that Nova knows the image is available and ready to use. We can check this through the EC2 API with the *euca-describe-images* utility. Make sure you've sourced your user credentials before executing this command.

```
# euca-describe-images
IMAGE  aki-7eea4179 images/natty-server-uec-amd64-vmlinuz-virtual.manifest.xml
available public x86_64 kernel
IMAGE  ami-6683ba18 images/natty-server-uec-amd64.img.manifest.xml  available
public x86_64 machine aki-7eea4179
```

We can also check for images through the OpenStack API with the *nova* command-line tool.

```
$ nova image-list
+------------+------+--------+
|     ID     | Name | Status |
+------------+------+--------+
| 1719908888 | None | ACTIVE |
| 2129281401 | None | ACTIVE |
+------------+------+--------+
```

Launching Instances

Now that we have a valid user and virtual disk image, we are ready to launch our first Nova instance. But before we start spinning up instances, we need to make a keypair so that we will be able to log in to the new instance via ssh. To create your keypair, use the *euca-add-keypair* tool:

```
# euca-add-keypair ken > ken.pem
# chmod 600 ken.pem
```

Now that we have the key, let's launch an instance. Launching an instance via the EC2 API requires three arguments: your keypair name (not the filename "ken.pem", just "ken"), the size (although it will default to "m1.tiny"), and the machine image name (we'll use our previously uploaded "ami-6683ba18" image):

```
# euca-run-instances -k ken -t m1.tiny ami-6683ba18
RESERVATION    r-1pkchwbm book default
INSTANCE    i-00000001 ami-6683ba18 scheduling ken (book, None) 0 m1.tiny
2011-07-04T20:28:51Z unknown zone
```

As you can see from the output from *euca-run-instances*, our instance has been launched and it is currently in the 'scheduling' state. If we wait a few minutes and everything goes well, it should progress to the 'running' state. We can check on its progress through the EC2 API with the *euca-describe-instances* command:

```
# euca-describe-instances
RESERVATION    r-1pkchwbm book default
INSTANCE    i-00000001 ami-6683ba18 10.0.0.2  10.0.0.2  running
ken (book, nova-controller) 0 m1.tiny  2011-07-04T20:28:51Z nova
```

We can also use the *nova* utility to make the same query through the OpenStack API. With this tool, you are looking for the 'ACTIVE' status:

```
# nova list
+----+----------+--------+---------------+------------+
| ID |   Name   | Status |   Public IP   | Private IP |
+----+----------+--------+---------------+------------+
| 1  | Server 1 | ACTIVE |               | 10.0.0.2   |
+----+----------+--------+---------------+------------+
```

 If your instance never makes it to 'ACTIVE' status or 'running' state after 10 minutes, something has mostly likely gone awry. Check the your logs (in this order) for *nova-api*, *nova-compute*, *nova-network*, and then *nova-scheduler*.

Configuring Network Connectivity

With the instance up and running, we now need to configure network access to it. This is a two-step process: first, we need to permit traffic to the instance, and then we need to associate a public IP address to it. Without configuring network access to it, you won't be able to access it from outside of the Nova. In this example, we will permit *SSH* (TCP port 22) and ICMP traffic to our instance from any IP address.

```
# euca-authorize default -P tcp -p 22 -s 0.0.0.0/0
GROUP default
PERMISSION default ALLOWS tcp 22 22 FROM CIDR 0.0.0.0/0
# euca-authorize default -P icmp -t -1:-1
GROUP default
PERMISSION default ALLOWS icmp -1 -1
```

 Realize that we've only permitted basic access to the instance. If you want to communicate with the server beyond *ping* and *SSH*, you'll need to authorize additional ports. For example, to allow for web server traffic, you will need to authorize TCP port 80.

With traffic permitted to the instance, we now need to assign a public address to it. This is also a two-step process: allocate an address and then associate it to our instance.

```
# euca-allocate-address
ADDRESS     192.168.1.128
# euca-associate-address -i i-00000001 192.168.1.128
ADDRESS     192.168.1.128 i-00000001
# nova list
+----+----------+--------+---------------+------------+
| ID |   Name   | Status |   Public IP   | Private IP |
+----+----------+--------+---------------+------------+
| 1  | Server 1 | ACTIVE | 192.168.1.128 | 10.0.0.2   |
+----+----------+--------+---------------+------------+
```

Public addressing operates differently on Nova than on Amazon EC2. EC2 automatically assigns each instance a public and private address (floating and fixed addresses in Nova). Nova automatically assigns a private address but requires manual allocation of a public address.

Accessing Instances

With network access completely configured, we are finally able to log in to our instance. Our image has been set up with *SSH* access secured with our keypair. Use *SSH* with our keypair filename (ken.pem), along with our username (which is "ubuntu" for this image) and the public IP address from our last step (192.168.1.128 in this example):

```
# ssh -i ken.pem ubuntu@192.168.1.128
Welcome to Ubuntu 11.04 (GNU/Linux 2.6.38-8-virtual x86_64)

 * Documentation:  https://help.ubuntu.com/

  System information as of Tue Jul  5 04:12:18 UTC 2011

  System load:  0.0               Processes:           61
  Usage of /:   41.5% of 1.35GB   Users logged in:     0
  Memory usage: 19%               IP address for eth0: 10.0.0.2
  Swap usage:   0%

  Graph this data and manage this system at https://landscape.canonical.com/
-------------------------------------------------------------------
At the moment, only the core of the system is installed. To tune the
system to your needs, you can choose to install one or more
predefined collections of software by running the following
command:

    sudo tasksel --section server
-------------------------------------------------------------------
Last login: Mon Jul  4 23:50:50 2011 from 192.168.1.67
ubuntu@i-00000001:~$
```

Congratulations! You have installed your cloud, configured it for use, and launched your first virtual machine.

At this point, you can deploy your applications and use it as any other server. But before we finish, let's do a few more things.

Attaching Volumes

Let's create our first volume. This is a straightforward *euca-create-volume* with the arguments -s 1 (for the size of the volume in gigabytes) and -z nova (which is nova as the default) for the zone. It will return with the volume name and its status (creating). You can check on the status with the *euca-describe-volumes*.

```
$ euca-create-volume -s 1 -z nova
VOLUME    vol-00000003    1    creating (book, None, None, None)
2011-07-11T00:08:34Z
```

 Volumes are only currently supported with the Amazon EC2 API. As
such, you will need to use euca2ools if you want to use volumes with
your instances.

Once the volume has been created, attach it to a running instance with the *euca-attach-volume*.

```
# euca-attach-volume vol-00000003 -i  i-00000004 -d /dev/vdb
VOLUME    vol-00000003
# euca-describe-volumes
VOLUME    vol-00000001    1         nova    error (book, nova-controller, None, None)
2011-07-10T22:55:28Z
VOLUME    vol-00000002    1         nova    error (book, nova-controller, None, None)
2011-07-10T22:57:02Z
VOLUME    vol-00000003    1         nova    in-use (book, nova-controller,
i-00000004[nova-controller], /dev/vdb)    2011-07-11T00:08:34Z
```

Volumes will show up as raw devices at */dev/vdb*. As with any raw device, you will need to make a filesystem on it and then mount it.

```
$ df -h
Filesystem         Size  Used Avail Use% Mounted on
/dev/vda           1.4G  549M  767M  42% /
devtmpfs           246M  144K  245M   1% /dev
none               247M     0  247M   0% /dev/shm
none               247M   40K  247M   1% /var/run
none               247M     0  247M   0% /var/lock
$ sudo mkdir /volumes
$ sudo mkfs -t ext3 /dev/vdb
$ sudo mount /dev/vdb /volumes
$ df -h
Filesystem         Size  Used Avail Use% Mounted on
/dev/vda           1.4G  549M  767M  42% /
devtmpfs           246M  144K  245M   1% /dev
none               247M     0  247M   0% /dev/shm
none               247M   40K  247M   1% /var/run
none               247M     0  247M   0% /var/lock
/dev/vdb          1008M   34M  924M   4% /volumes
```

 Volumes may only be attached to one instance at a time. Volumes cannot be shared between instances concurrently.

Once you are done using the volume, you can *umount* the volume as any other. Now
that the volume is no longer mounted on our instance, we can safely detach it with the
euca-detach-volume.

```
$ sudo umount /volumes
ubuntu@i-00000004:~$ df -h
Filesystem       Size  Used Avail Use% Mounted on
/dev/vda         1.4G  549M  767M  42% /
devtmpfs         246M  144K  245M   1% /dev
none             247M     0  247M   0% /dev/shm
none             247M   40K  247M   1% /var/run
none             247M     0  247M   0% /var/lock
# euca-describe-volumes
VOLUME     vol-00000003  1 nova in-use
(book, nova-controller, i-00000004[nova-controller], /dev/vdb) 2011-07-11T00:08:34Z
# euca-detach-volume vol-00000003
VOLUME     vol-00000003
# euca-describe-volumes
VOLUME     vol-00000003 1 nova available (book, nova-controller, None, None)
    2011-07-11T00:08:34Z
```

Finally, you can completely destroy the detached volume with the *euca-delete-volume*. This will take a while, as the volume will be completely zeroed out to prevent other users from seeing this data.

```
# euca-describe-volumes
VOLUME     vol-00000003 1 nova available (book, nova-controller, None, None)
    2011-07-11T00:08:34Z
# euca-delete-volume vol-00000003
VOLUME     vol-00000003
# euca-describe-volumes
VOLUME     vol-00000003 1 nova deleting (book, nova-controller, None, None)
    2011-07-11T00:08:34Z
# euca-describe-volumes
#
```

Terminating Instances

Instances can be ended with the *euca-terminate-instances*. It accepts one or more instance ids as arguments.

```
$ euca-describe-instances
RESERVATION    r-9puzwes7  book  default
INSTANCE   i-00000004  ami-6683ba18  10.0.0.2 10.0.0.2 running
ken (book, nova-controller) 0  m1.tiny 2011-07-11T00:10:42Z nova
# euca-terminate-instances i-00000004
# euca-describe-instances
```

 Simply shutting down or powering off an instance does not terminate it in Nova. You need to actually use the *euca-terminate-instances* command to release their resources. This is different behavior than you may be used to from Amazon EC2.

## CHAPTER 9

Administering Nova

Nova has a myriad of configuration options due to its wide support of differing technologies, products, and architectures. This section gives you an overview of the most important configuration options, as well as important administrative commands to bend Nova to your will.

Configuration Files

Nova daemons are given configuration options on startup through a set of flags usually set in text file. Traditionally, this file is located at *etc/nova.conf*. However, these flags can also be set directly on the command line or in an alternate configuration file that is designated at run time.

> To use an alternate configuration file with the a Nova daemon, simply make the file path the argument to the *--flagfile=/path/to/altnova.conf* flag. To pass arbitrary flags on the command line, simply include them and they will override the values in the configuration file.

The *etc/nova.conf* file is a very simple format: put each flag on a separate line, with no comments or other characters. Here is an example of a minimal *etc/nova.conf* file:

```
--sql_connection=mysql://root:nova@localhost/nova
--auth_driver=nova.auth.dbdriver.DbDriver
--daemonize=1
--fixed_range=172.16.0.0/24
--network_size=32
```

> One of the weaknesses of Nova is that the *etc/nova.conf* does not not support comments. All lines in the file are evaluated. As such, it does not include any helpful configuration comments that you might see in other open source packages.

The most complete list of Nova configuration flags is maintained at *http://wiki.open
stack.org/FlagsGrouping*. Please note that this last sentence said "most complete," not
"definitive." The definitive source of all configuration flags is the Nova source code.

Configuration Tools

Nova administration is accomplished through a tool called *nova-manage*. Most commands take the form *nova-manage* command subcommand and any necessary arguments.
At any time, you can see help for *nova-manage* by leaving off any arguments, subcommands, or commands. Here is an example of finding help for creating a new user:

```
$ nova-manage
nova-manage category action [<args>]
Available categories:
    user
    account
    project
    role
    shell
    vpn
    fixed
    floating
    network
    vm
    service
    db
    volume
    instance_type
    image
    flavor
$ nova-manage user
nova-manage category action [<args>]
Available actions for user category:
    admin
    create
    delete
    exports
    list
    modify
    revoke
$ nova-manage user create
Possible wrong number of arguments supplied
user create: creates a new user and prints exports
        arguments: name [access] [secret]
2011-07-15 18:55:13,520 CRITICAL nova [-] create() takes at least 2 arguments (1 given)
```

Do not worry about the error after the *nova-manage user create*—it is simply telling
you that you haven't supplied the necessary arguments.

Service

Services can be monitored through the *nova-manage* command on a service or host basis. With the *service*, you can either view or actively manage services. For example, you can query a host for the services that it currently offers, or simply list all the services that are available. This is an essential command for testing or troubleshooting your deployment. Below is an example that walks through the full array of of *service* sub-commands: listing services, enabling and disabling services, and describing resources on a host.

```
# nova-manage service list nova-controller nova-compute
nova-controller nova-compute enabled  :-) 2011-07-08 22:36:54
# nova-manage service disable nova-controller nova-scheduler
# nova-manage service list
nova-controller nova-compute enabled  :-) 2011-07-08 22:38:04
nova-controller nova-network enabled  XXX 2011-07-08 22:38:12
nova-controller nova-scheduler disabled :-) 2011-07-08 22:38:07
nova-controller nova-volume enabled  :-) 2011-07-08 22:38:07
# nova-manage service enable nova-controller nova-scheduler
# nova-manage service list
nova-controller nova-compute enabled  :-) 2011-07-08 22:38:24
nova-controller nova-network enabled  :-) 2011-07-08 22:38:22
nova-controller nova-scheduler enabled  :-) 2011-07-08 22:38:27
nova-controller nova-volume enabled  :-) 2011-07-08 22:38:27
# nova-manage service describe_resource nova-controller
HOST                  PROJECT    cpu    mem(mb)    disk(gb)
nova-controller(total)            2      3930       219
nova-controller(used)             0      368        12
nova-controller        book       1      512        0
```

nova-manage service also allows you to update resources that are available on a particular host. This is only applies to compute hosts.

Quotas

Nova can apply quotas on number of instances, total cores, total volumes, volume size, and other items on a per-project basis. Table 9-1 illustrates all quota options, their default values, and a brief description.

Table 9-1. Nova Quotas

Quota Flag	Default Value	Description
quota_instances	10	number of instances allowed per project
quota_cores	20	number of instance cores allowed per project
quota_volumes	10	number of volumes allowed per project
quota_gigabytes	1000	number of volume gigabytes allowed per project
quota_floating_ips	10	number of floating ips allowed per project
quota_metadata_items	128	number of metadata items allowed per instance

Quota Flag	Default Value	Description
quota_max_injected_files	5	number of injected files allowed
quota_max_injected_file_content_bytes	10 * 1024	number of bytes allowed per injected file
quota_max_injected_file_path_bytes	255	number of bytes allowed per injected file path

These default values for all projects are set in the source code (*nova/quota.py*) but can be overridden for all projects or individual projects. To override the default value for all projects, simply add the appropriate flag with a new value to the */etc/nova.conf* file. For example, to change the total cores available to each project, append this line to the */etc/nova.conf* file:

```
--quota_cores=100
```

It is also possible to adjust quotas on particular projects with the *nova-manage* command. To increase the total cores allotted to a mythical "payroll" project, execute the following command:

```
$ nova-manage project quota payroll cores 150
metadata_items: 128
gigabytes: 1000
floating_ips: 10
instances: 100
volumes: 10
cores: 150
```

 As you may have noticed, the flags for quotas (quota_cores) are different from the *nova-manage* command keys (cores). Using the flag in *nova-manage* or the *nova-manage* keys in */etc/nova.conf* will have no effect.

As you can see from the command listing above, we specified the project ("payroll"), then the quota key ("cores"), and finally the new value. Executing *nova-manage project quota payroll* without a key and value will print out a list of the current values for all quotas.

Database

The *nova-manage db* command is rarely used except for troubleshooting and upgrades. It has two subcommands: *sync* and *version*. The *sync* subcommand will upgrade the database scheme for new versions of Nova and the *version* will report the current version.

Nova uses a database abstraction library called SQL-Alchemy to interact with its database. A complimentary package called `sqlalchemy-migrate` is used to manage the database schema. Inspired by Ruby on Rails' migrations feature, it provides a programmatic way to handle database schema changes. For Nova administrators, this only applies when they are upgrading versions.

To upgrade scheme versions, use the *nova-manage db sync*. This should be rarely used unless you are installing from source or upgrading your installation. If there are pending scheme migrations, it will apply those to your database. If there are not, it will return nothing.

```
# nova-manage db sync
#
```

To view the database scheme version, use the *db version* arguments:

```
# nova-manage db version
14
```

The database version for Cactus is 14

Instance Types and Flavors

Instance types (or "flavors," as the OpenStack API calls them) are resources granted to instances in Nova. In more specific terms, this is the size of the instance (vCPUs, RAM, Storage, etc.) that will be launched. You may recognize these by the names "m1.large" or "m1.tiny" in Amazon Web Services EC2 parlance. The OpenStack API calls these "flavors" and they tend to have names like "256 MB Server."

Instance types or flavors are managed through *nova-manage* with the *instance_types* command and an appropriate subcommand. At the current time, instance type manipulation isn't exposed through the APIs nor the adminclient.

You can use the *flavor* command as a synonym for *instance_types* in any of these examples.

During installation, Nova creates five instance types that mirror the basic Amazon EC2 instance types. To see all currently active instance types, use the *list* subcommand:

```
$ nova-manage instance_type list
m1.medium: Memory: 4096MB, VCPUS: 2, Storage: 40GB, FlavorID: 3, Swap: 0GB,
RXTX Quota: 0GB, RXTX Cap: 0MB
```

```
m1.large: Memory: 8192MB, VCPUS: 4, Storage: 80GB, FlavorID: 4, Swap: 0GB,
RXTX Quota: 0GB, RXTX Cap: 0MB
m1.tiny: Memory: 512MB, VCPUS: 1, Storage: 0GB, FlavorID: 1, Swap: 0GB,
RXTX Quota: 0GB, RXTX Cap: 0MB
m1.xlarge: Memory: 16384MB, VCPUS: 8, Storage: 160GB, FlavorID: 5, Swap: 0GB,
RXTX Quota: 0GB, RXTX Cap: 0MB
m1.small: Memory: 2048MB, VCPUS: 1, Storage: 20GB, FlavorID: 2, Swap: 0GB,
RXTX Quota: 0GB, RXTX Cap: 0MB
```

Again, and just for emphasis, you could just as easily have used the *flavor* subcommand to get the exact same output:

```
$ nova-manage flavor list
m1.medium: Memory: 4096MB, VCPUS: 2, Storage: 40GB, FlavorID: 3, Swap: 0GB,
RXTX Quota: 0GB, RXTX Cap: 0MB
m1.large: Memory: 8192MB, VCPUS: 4, Storage: 80GB, FlavorID: 4, Swap: 0GB,
RXTX Quota: 0GB, RXTX Cap: 0MB
m1.tiny: Memory: 512MB, VCPUS: 1, Storage: 0GB, FlavorID: 1, Swap: 0GB,
RXTX Quota: 0GB, RXTX Cap: 0MB
m1.xlarge: Memory: 16384MB, VCPUS: 8, Storage: 160GB, FlavorID: 5, Swap: 0GB,
RXTX Quota: 0GB, RXTX Cap: 0MB
m1.small: Memory: 2048MB, VCPUS: 1, Storage: 20GB, FlavorID: 2, Swap: 0GB,
RXTX Quota: 0GB, RXTX Cap: 0MB
```

To create an instance type, use the *create* subcommand with the following positional arguments:

- Memory (expressed in megabytes)
- vCPU(s) (integer)
- Local storage (expressed in gigabytes)
- Flavorid (unique integer)
- Swap space (expressed in megabytes, defaults to zero, optional)
- RXTX quotas (expressed in gigabytes, defaults to zero, optional)
- RXTX cap (expressed in gigabytes, defaults to zero, optional)

The following example creates an instance type named "m1.xxlarge":

```
$ nova-manage instance_type create m1.xxlarge 32768 16 320 0 0 0
m1.xxlarge created
```

To delete an instance type, use the *delete* subcommand and specify the name:

```
$ nova-manage instance_type delete m1.xxlarge
m1.xxlarge deleted
```

Note that the *delete* command only marks the instance type as inactive in the database; it does not actually remove the instance type. This is done to preserve the instance type definition for long running instances (which may not terminate for months or years). If you are sure that you want to delete this instance type from the database, pass the *--purge* flag after the name:

```
$ nova-manage instance_type delete m1.xxlarge --purge
m1.xxlarge purged
```

Be careful with deleting instance types, as you might need this information later. This is especially true in commercial or enterprise environments where you might be creating a bill based off the instance type's name or configuration. Unless you truly need to prune the size of your instance_types table, you are much safer to just *delete* the instance type.

Virtual Machine

Nova also lets you query all the current running virtual machines, similar to how the OpenStack API or EC2 API does with their tools.

```
# nova-manage vm list
instance   node          type      state     launched              image
kernel     ramdisk       project   user      zone       index
i-00000003 nova-controller nova.db.sqlalchemy.models.InstanceTypes object at
0x429c910 launching  None    1719908888  2129281401   book      ken
None       0
```

 There is a bug in *nova-manage vm list* in Cactus where it cannot properly decipher the instance type (the type field above). This is corrected in the upcoming version of the Nova.

nova-manage vm also has an advanced KVM feature called *live_migration*. Live migration allows you to move virtual machine instances between hosts if the following conditions are met:

- KVM or QEMU is the virtualization technology
- The volume driver is iSCSI or AoE

Live migration is invoked with an instance id and destination host as arguments:

```
# nova-manage live_migration i-00000003 new-host
Migration of i-00000003 initiated. Check its progress using euca-describe-instances.
```

Network

Nova has a trio of *nova-manage* networking commands: network, fixed, and floating. The *nova-manage network* is the most powerful. It allows you to list, create, and delete networks within the Nova database. For example:

```
# nova-manage network list
network       netmask          start address  DNS
10.0.0.0/25   255.255.255.128  10.0.0.2       8.8.4.4
```

The *fixed* command simply allows you to view the fixed IP address mappings to hostname, host, and MAC address. Here are the truncated results of the command (it goes on to show the every IP address in the mapping):

```
# nova-manage fixed list
network       IP address    MAC address    hostname    host
10.0.0.0/25   10.0.0.0      None           None        None
```

10.0.0.0/25	10.0.0.1	None	None	None
10.0.0.0/25	10.0.0.2	02:16:3e:5f:bc:a7	i-00000003	nova-controller
10.0.0.0/25	10.0.0.3	None	None	None
10.0.0.0/25	10.0.0.4	None	None	None
10.0.0.0/25	10.0.0.5	None	None	None
10.0.0.0/25	10.0.0.6	None	None	None

The *floating* command is very similar to the *fixed* command except that it manipulates public IP addresses. The example below creates a floating range and then shows their allocation.

```
# nova-manage float create cactus 192.168.1.128/29
# nova-manage float list
cactus    192.168.1.128 None
cactus    192.168.1.129 None
cactus    192.168.1.130 None
cactus    192.168.1.131 None
cactus    192.168.1.132 None
cactus    192.168.1.133 None
cactus    192.168.1.134 None
cactus    192.168.1.135 None
```

Shell

As purely a troubleshooting command, *nova-manage shell* allows you to start up a Nova environment so that you can issue ad hoc Python commands. You might use this to discover your installed version:

```
# nova-manage shell python
Python 2.6.5 (r265:79063, Apr 16 2010, 13:57:41)
[GCC 4.4.3] on linux2
Type "help", "copyright", "credits" or "license" for more information.
(InteractiveConsole)
>>> from nova import version
>>> version.version_string()
'2011.2'
>>> version.version_string_with_vcs()
u'2011.2-LOCALBRANCH:LOCALREVISION'
>>> exit()
```

While I have used the basic shell in this example, you can also invoke the *bpython* or *ipython* shells. *nova-manage shell* can also be used for more elaborate troubleshooting scenarios depending on your Nova internals knowledge.

Volumes

The volume command for *nova-manage* should only be used when traditional methods have failed. It supports two subcommands: *reattach* and *delete*. While both subcommands are fairly self-explanatory, the situations where they are applicable may not be.

The *delete* subcommand should only be used when traditional methods of removing it has failed. As an example, we will delete a volume that has been marked in the "error" state:

```
# euca-describe-volumes
VOLUME    vol-00000002  1  nova error (book, nova-controller, None, None)
    2011-07-10T22:57:02Z
VOLUME    vol-00000003  1  nova available (book, nova-controller, None, None)
    2011-07-11T00:08:34Z
# nova-manage volume delete vol-00000002
# euca-describe-volumes
VOLUME    vol-00000003  1 nova available (book, nova-controller, None, None)
    2011-07-11T00:08:34Z
```

 This subcommand will not let you delete a volume that is marked with the status "in-use" (which would mean that it is attached to an instance). You will need to detach the volume from the instance before trying this subcommand.

The *reattach* command allows you to reconnect a volume to an instance. Most likely, this will only need to be used after a compute host has been rebooted.

About the Author

Ken Pepple currently serves as the Director of Cloud Development at Internap, where he leads the engineering of their OpenStack-based cloud service. Previously, he held technical leadership positions at Sun Microsystems and Oracle, including Chief Technologist for their Systems Line of Business and Technical Director for their Asia Pacific consulting organization.

You can contact Ken and see his current work at his blog: *http://ken.pepple.info*.

Colophon

The animal on the cover of *Deploying OpenStack* is a Tenrec.

The cover image is from Cassell's *Natural History*. The cover font is Adobe ITC Garamond. The text font is Linotype Birka; the heading font is Adobe Myriad Condensed; and the code font is LucasFont's TheSansMonoCondensed.

Get even more
for your money.

Join the O'Reilly Community, and register the O'Reilly books you own. It's free, and you'll get:

- $4.99 ebook upgrade offer
- 40% upgrade offer on O'Reilly print books
- Membership discounts on books and events
- Free lifetime updates to ebooks and videos
- Multiple ebook formats, DRM FREE
- Participation in the O'Reilly community
- Newsletters
- Account management
- 100% Satisfaction Guarantee

Signing up is easy:

1. **Go to: oreilly.com/go/register**
2. **Create an O'Reilly login.**
3. **Provide your address.**
4. **Register your books.**

Note: English-language books only

To order books online:
oreilly.com/store

For questions about products or an order:
orders@oreilly.com

To sign up to get topic-specific email announcements and/or news about upcoming books, conferences, special offers, and new technologies:
elists@oreilly.com

For technical questions about book content:
booktech@oreilly.com

To submit new book proposals to our editors:
proposals@oreilly.com

O'Reilly books are available in multiple DRM-free ebook formats. For more information:
oreilly.com/ebooks

O'REILLY®

Spreading the knowledge of innovators   oreilly.com

The information you need, when and where you need it.

With Safari Books Online, you can:

Access the contents of thousands of technology and business books

- Quickly search over 7000 books and certification guides
- Download whole books or chapters in PDF format, at no extra cost, to print or read on the go
- Copy and paste code
- Save up to 35% on O'Reilly print books
- **New!** Access mobile-friendly books directly from cell phones and mobile devices

Stay up-to-date on emerging topics before the books are published

- Get on-demand access to evolving manuscripts.
- Interact directly with authors of upcoming books

Explore thousands of hours of video on technology and design topics

- Learn from expert video tutorials
- Watch and replay recorded conference sessions

Spreading the knowledge of innovators   safari.oreilly.com